FOR BETTY BOSTON -
CHAMPION OF THE
ARTS!

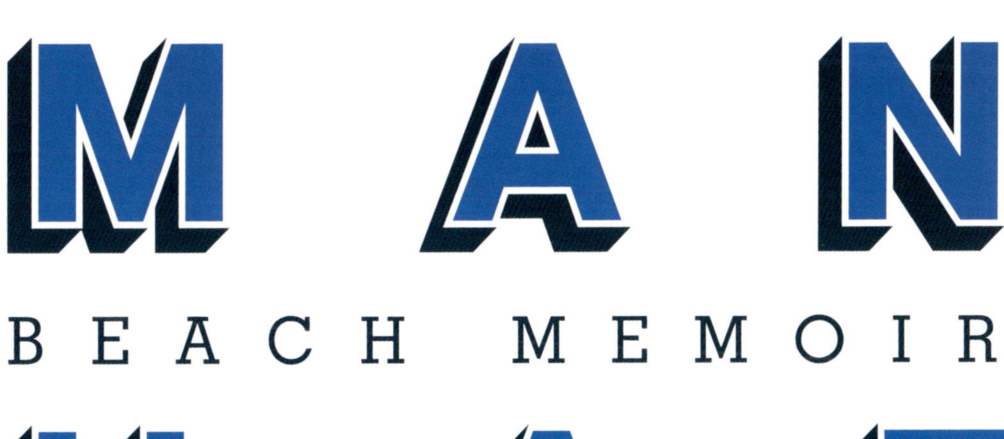

BEACH MEMOIR

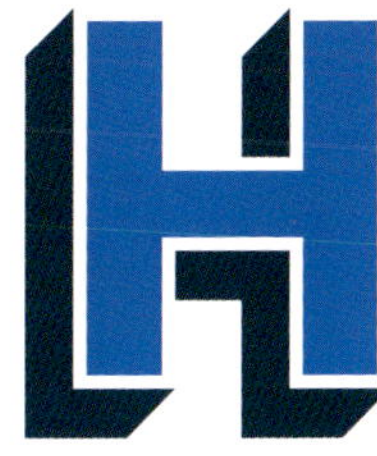

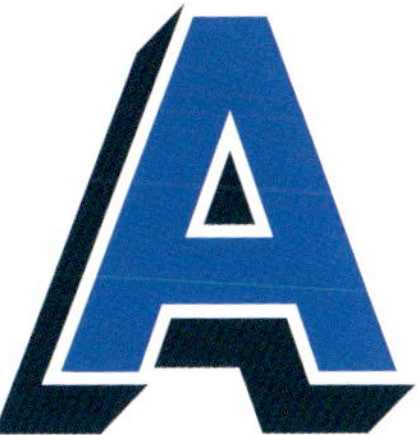

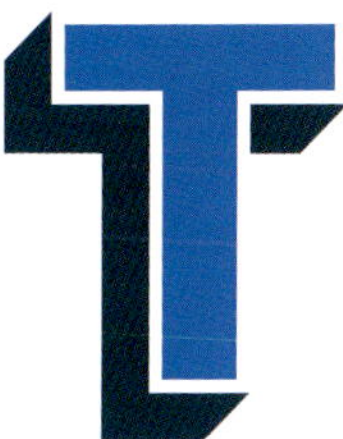

ARTIST GARY SWEENEY

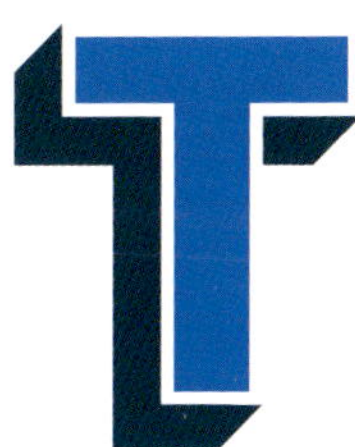

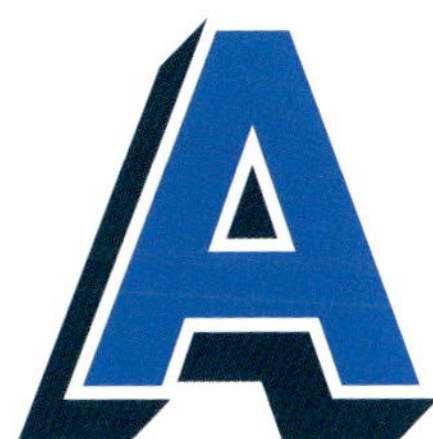

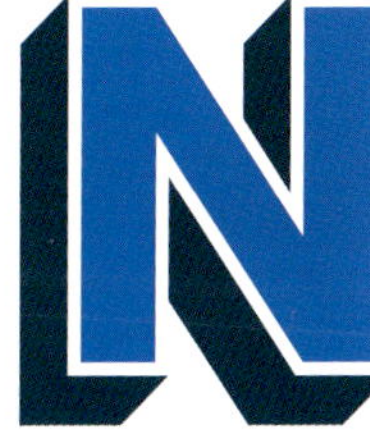

SAYS GOODBYE TO HIS CHILDHOOD HOME

Manhattan Beach Memoir: Artist Gary Sweeney Says Goodbye to His Childhood Home

Published by Stray Bird Publishing
New Orleans, Louisiana 70119

Book design by Andréa Caillouet
Photography by Gary Sweeney, Mike Sweeney, Walley Films, Paul Jonason, and courtesy of Manhattan Beach Historic Society

Editor, Andréa Caillouet
Copy Editor, Leigh M. Baldwin

978-0-692-15349-9 (Hardcover)
Printed in China

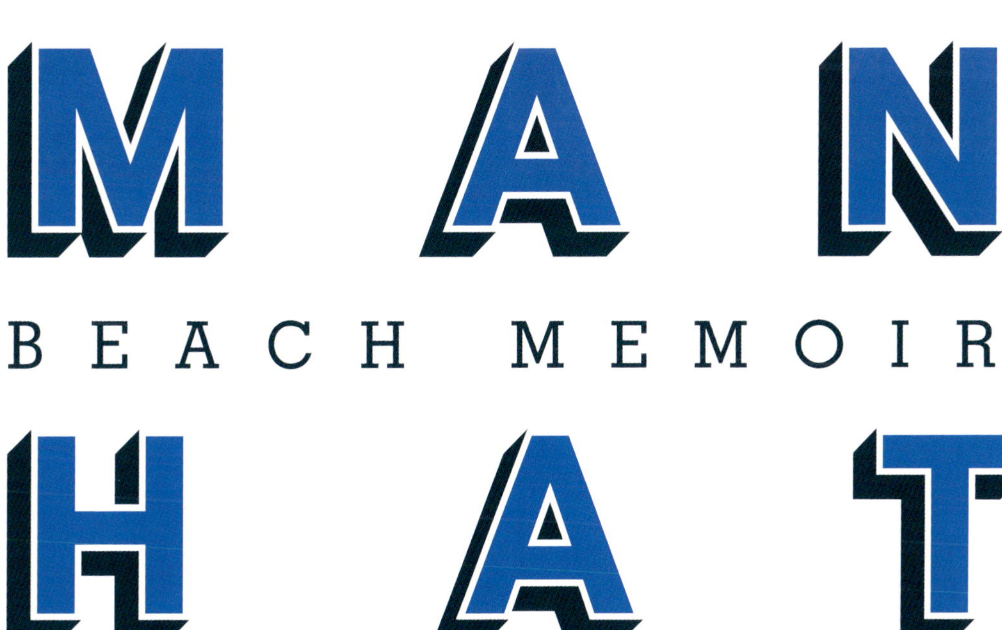

MAN
BEACH MEMOIR
HAT

ARTIST GARY SWEENEY

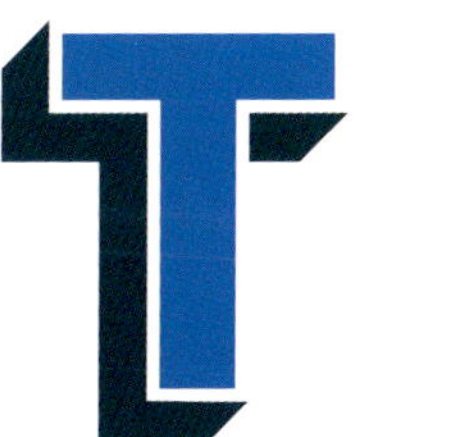 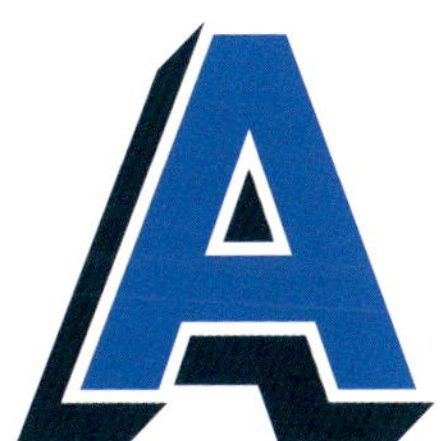 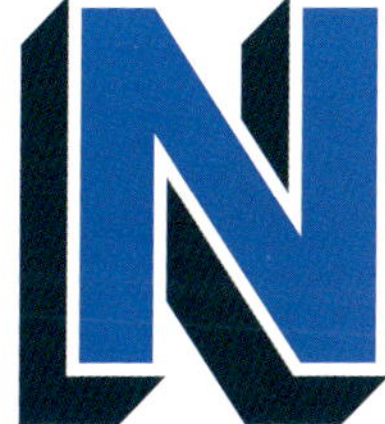

TAN

SAYS GOODBYE TO HIS CHILDHOOD HOME

Essays by WENDY WEIL ATWELL and NEIL FAUERSO

To my wife, Janet, who works tirelessly behind the scenes,
without credit, to make all of my efforts possible

And to our house at 320 35th Street,
our extended family who shared the house,
and the Manhattan Beach of my youth

Contents

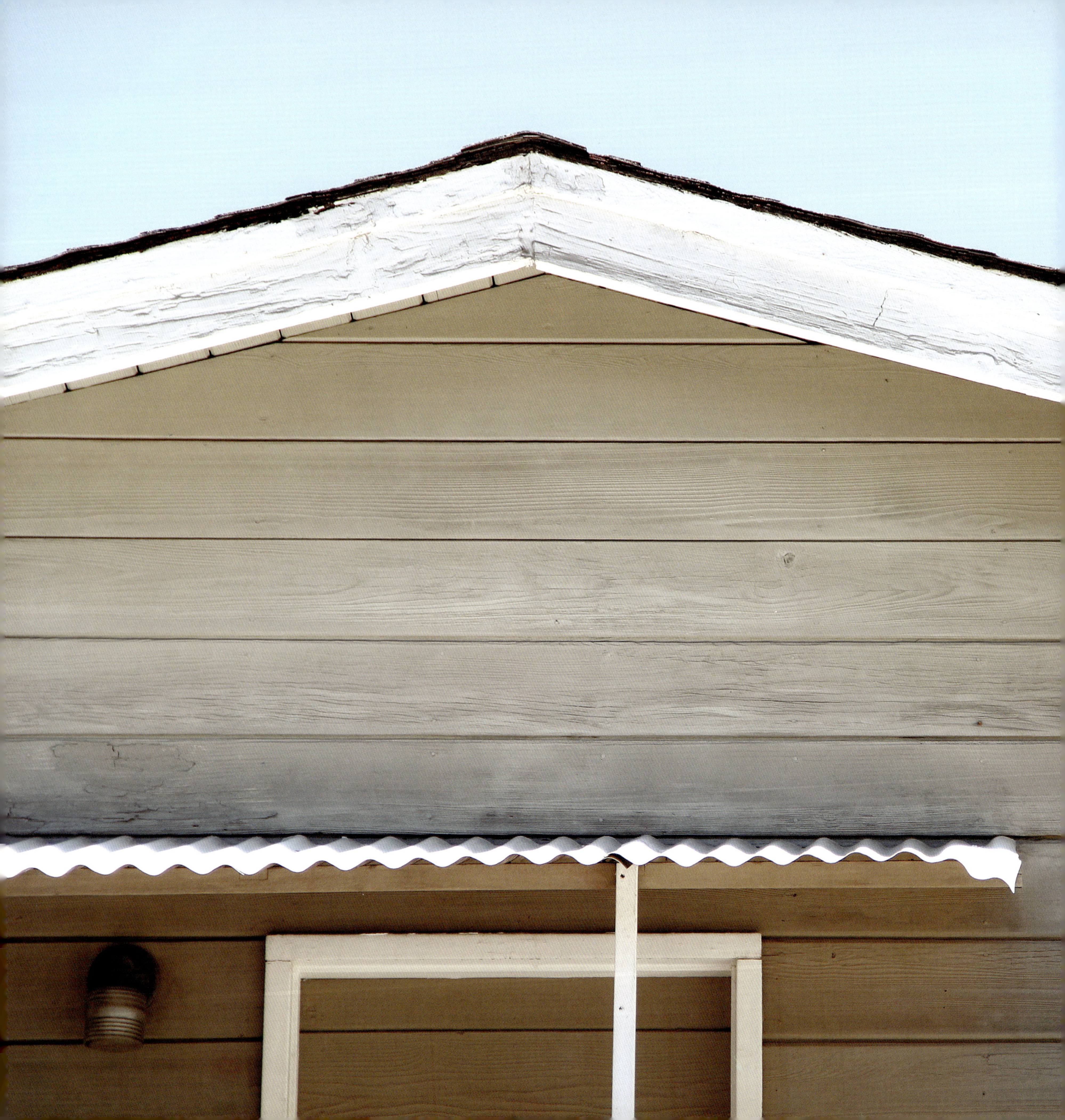

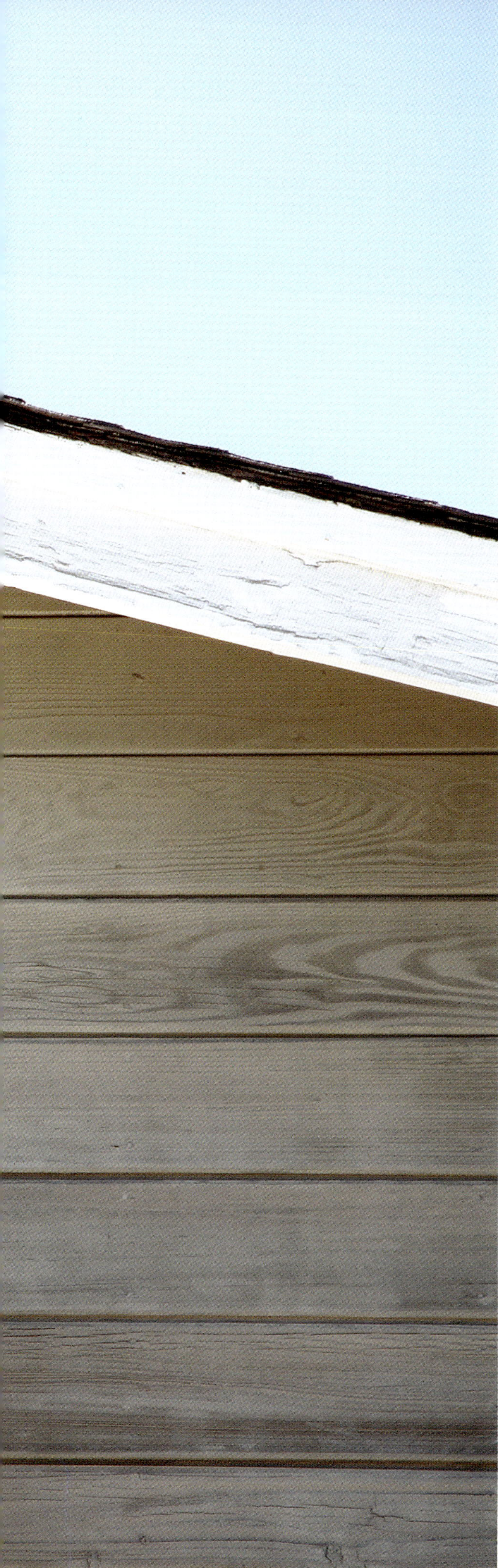

Rising Tides

Neil Fauerso

Michel Houellebecq writes: "The past is always beautiful. So, for that matter, is the future. Only the present hurts, and we carry it around like an abscess of suffering, our compassion between two infinities of happiness and peace." [1] This quote obviously reduces the horror of history and the dread of the future, but contains much truth, in particular for the post-World War II generation, especially if they happened to be white, male, and born and raised on the West Coast. For men like my father who was born and raised in the Bay Area and artist Gary Sweeney who was born and raised in Manhattan Beach—both in the 1950s and 1960s—they hit on what was probably the pinnacle of American middle-class living. For a few brief decades, the California paradise of ocean views, sea breezes through the trees, and bloomed sunsets that hang like remnants of fireworks, was shockingly affordable. Sweeney's mother bought his family's Manhattan Beach house fully furnished in 1945 for $5,400; 70 years later Gary would finally sell it when offered what he described as "two armored trucks full of money." One of the things the hippies and counterculture of the '60s and '70s—including Thomas Pynchon, who lived in Manhattan Beach while writing *Gravity's Rainbow*—underestimated even in their satire was the scale of the behemoth of the global market. Joni Mitchell was wrong when she sang, "They paved paradise and put in a parking lot." The property of paradise is far too valuable for a simple parking lot. When Neil Young sang, "Look out Mama, there's a white boat coming up the river," he didn't know that the white boat was an oligarch's 700-million-dollar private yacht, and it would blot out the sun.

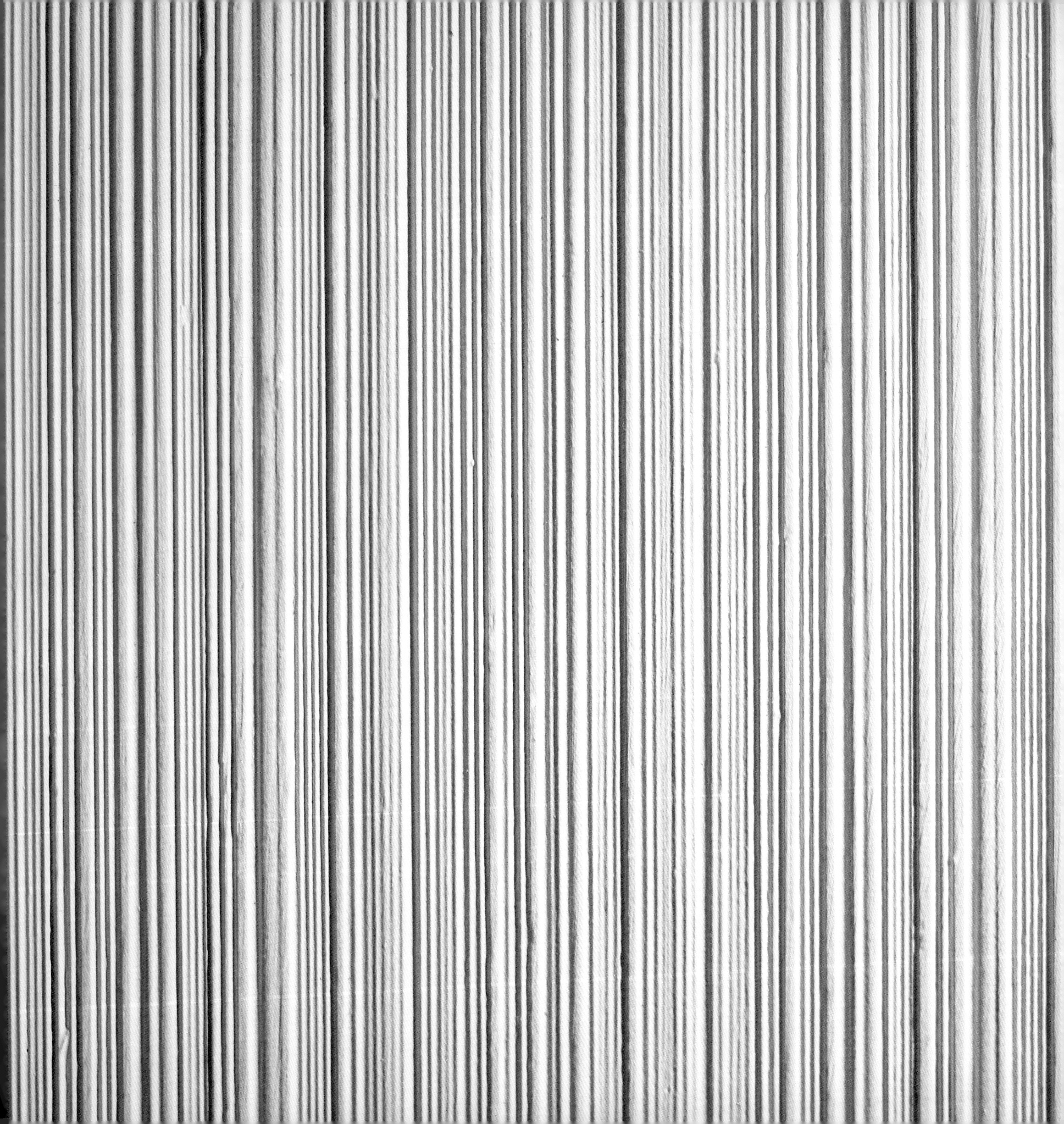

Gary's father Mike was, much like my own grandfather, an active presence in his local community. Such engaged relationship to one's home, similar to buying a house near the beach in Southern California for $5,400, seems to be a relic of a time temporarily removed from the churning forever struggle of the present. My grandfather, Walter Fauerso, worked for Chevron and in his spare time, planted around 100,000 trees and spearheaded a campaign to save an esteemed Richmond natatorium called The Plunge. Mike Sweeney owned a hardware store, served on Manhattan Beach's city council and as mayor, and was a very serious and accomplished amateur photographer. With these decades of photos, Gary created a tapestry on his home before it was razed by wealthy developers, narrating his upbringing. Gary's blond hair and wide grin personify a certain theatrical Americanness—to look at the pictures of Gary's idyllic, archetypal childhood covering the house is to be hit with a lattice work of cultural associations: *A Christmas Story, The Endless Summer,* vintage advertisements for National Parks. The effect of the installation is of course nostalgic, but steeped in such a surreal ambiance as to become a confounding dream. Gary did not grow up to become a company man or the mayor of his hometown; he became an artist who rode his bike across the US and eventually covered his childhood home in pictures, before a developer tore it down to build his dojo.

Kevin Cody's series "Ultrafication" chronicles the manic increases in the real estate market in Southern California. In Manhattan Beach, houses began selling for ten and then fifteen million dollars, as if the wind picked up the world, the line buckled and a deep sea fish escaped. In 2015, the median price of the three most expensive houses in Manhattan Beach was 15 million dollars, an increase of 86% in five years. For all homes, the median price increased by 50% in the same period to 2.1 million. Such increases create the fervor and desperation of a gold rush; what does living become if you're just waiting to sell?

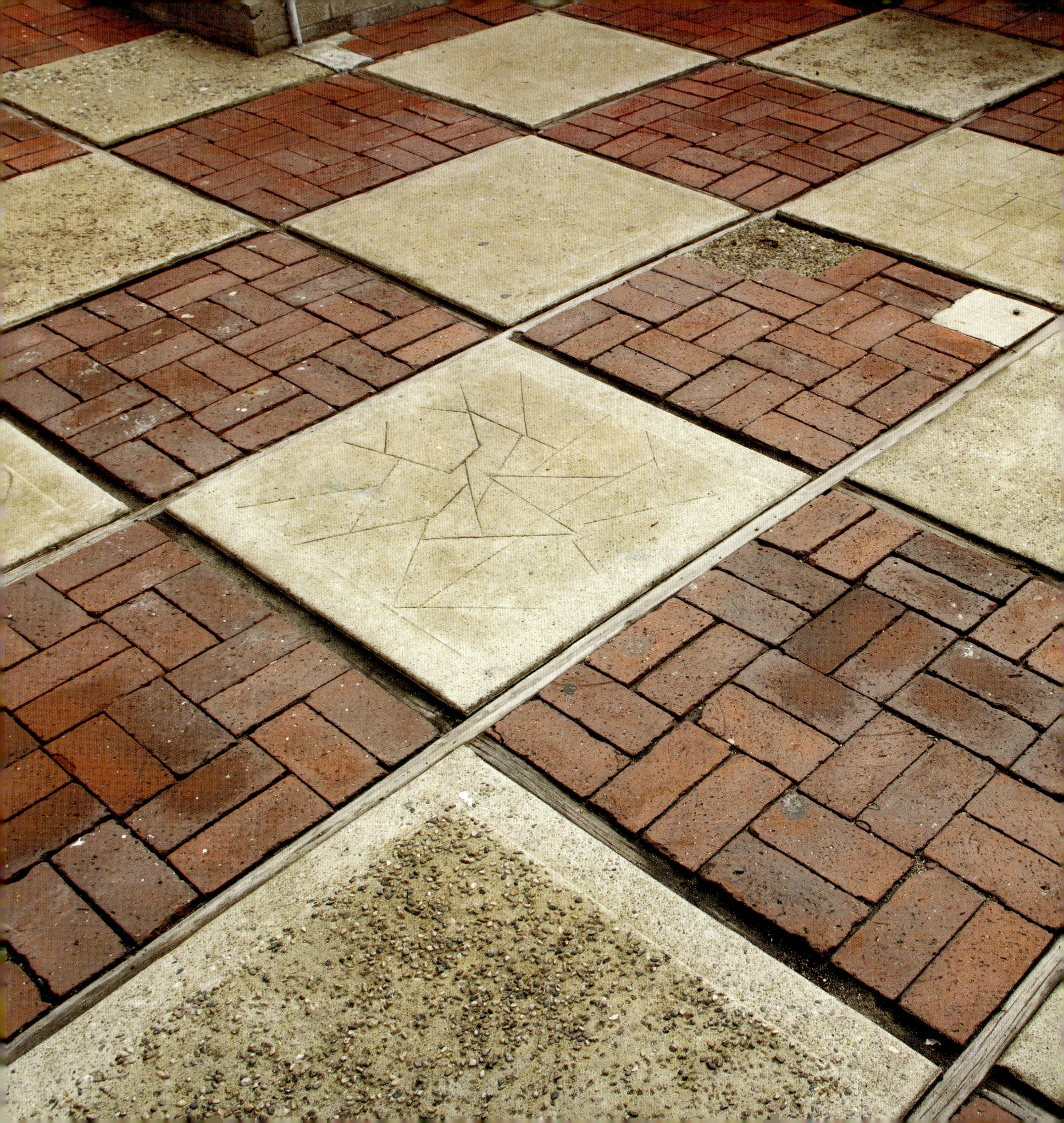

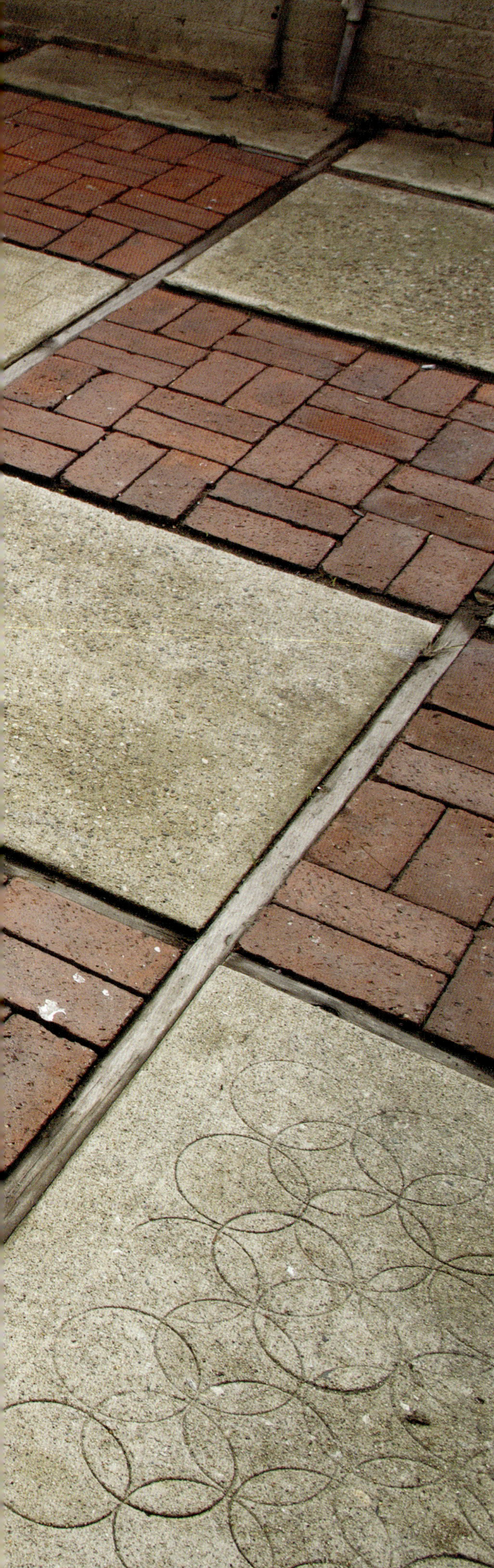

Discussing the coveted properties on Strand/Ocean Drive, Cody notes: "In Manhattan there are 173 Strand/Ocean Drive street addresses. The owners of 68 of these properties, or 39 percent, according to Carew's research, do not use Strand mailing addresses. The assumption that Strand homes with non-Strand owner addresses are not primary residences isn't 100 percent reliable. But assuming a 50 percent margin of error, it still suggests nearly one in five homes on the 2.3 mile long Manhattan Beach Strand are vacation homes or rentals." [2] Or, perhaps, in some cases they're not used at all, the receptacle for some international oligarch's suspiciously begotten funds. The more expensive a place becomes, the more empty it is.

One paragraph in particular stands out in Cody's piece: "An anomaly among the statistics is the change in median household income. According to U.S. Census data, it rose just two percent between 2010 and 2015, from $139,000 to $142,000, suggesting that the ultra-wealthy's impact on the city is disproportionate to their numbers." How could this be? It is akin to looking in the mirror and seeing strings. It is difficult to see a coherent future. What will happen to the new eight-figure houses? Will a patrician ultra-class so removed from the rest of the population as to become essentially aliens buy them, tear them down, and build nine-figure houses that slope over the horizon? It feels like a dream, but this has actually always been the world, rapacious, relentless, and sped up the way they play sitcoms so they can squeeze in one more ad. The dreams were those halcyon decades when you could run a hardware store and live on the beach and build your own darkroom. This dream may appear briefly as real once every hundred years, or it may only have happened once and will never come true again.

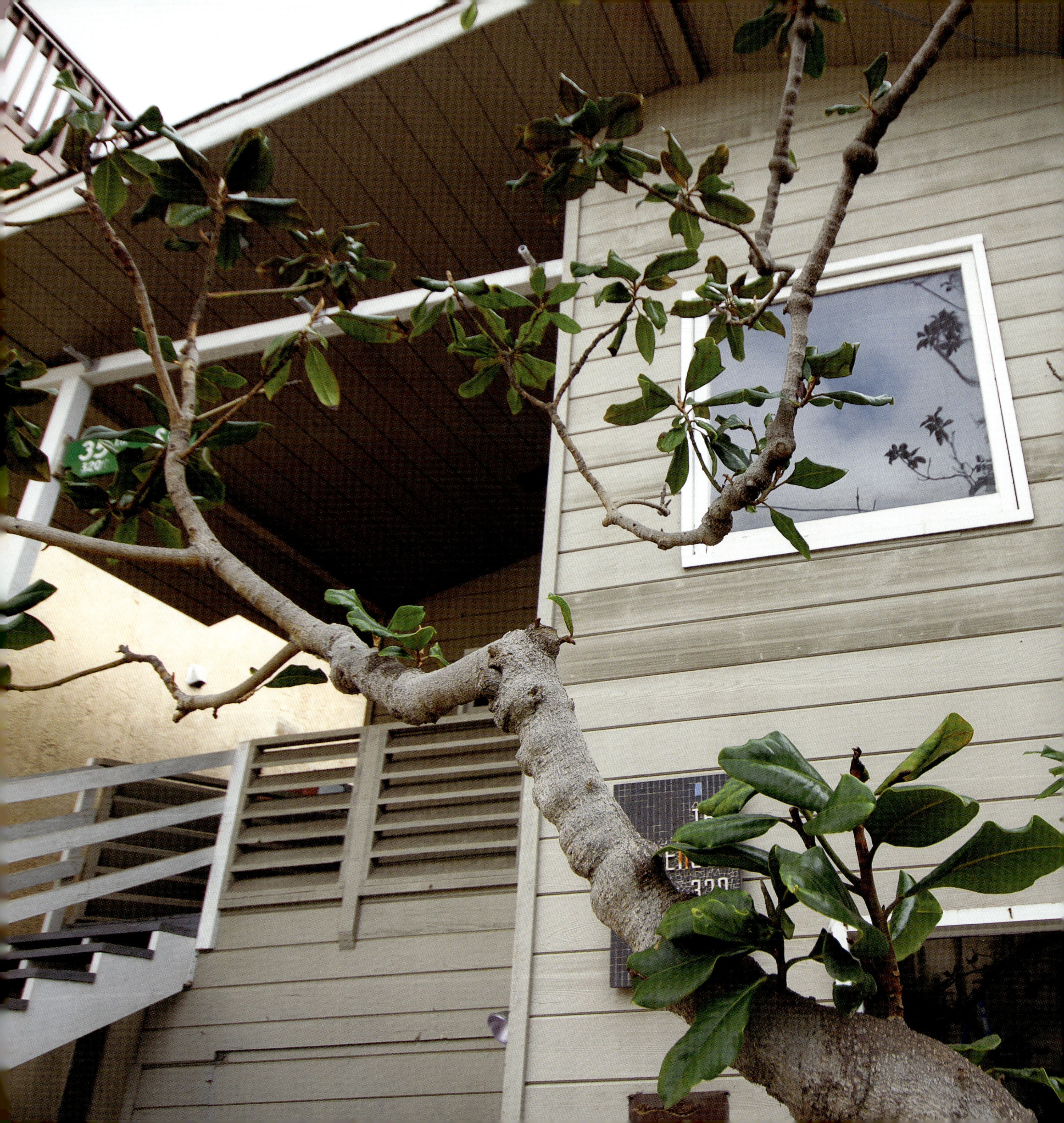

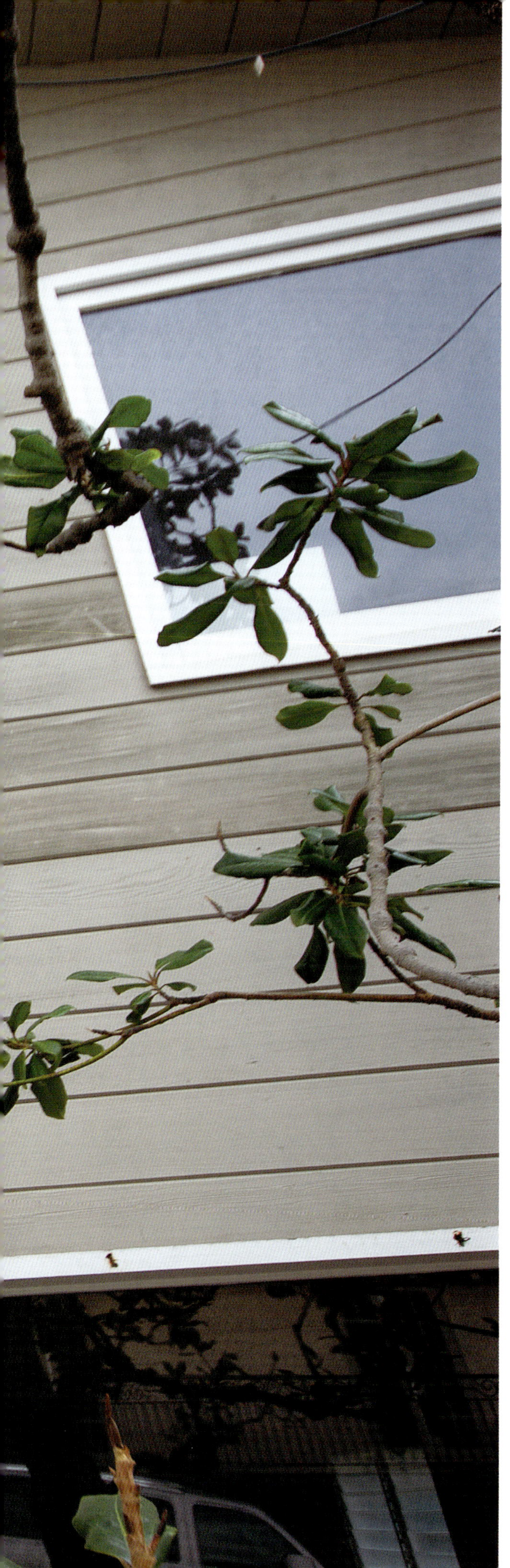

SUNSET
ON MANHATTAN BEACH

Wendy Weil Atwell

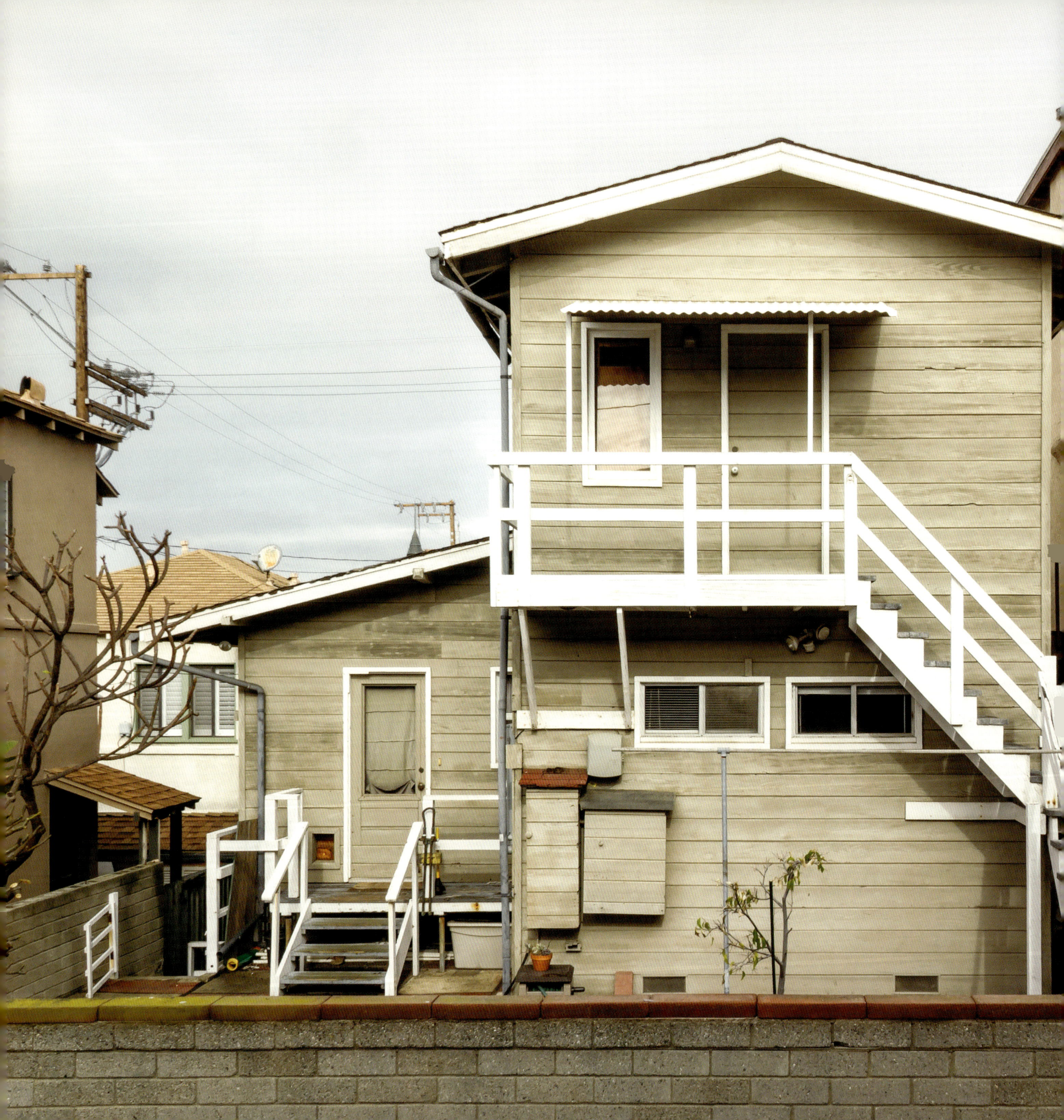

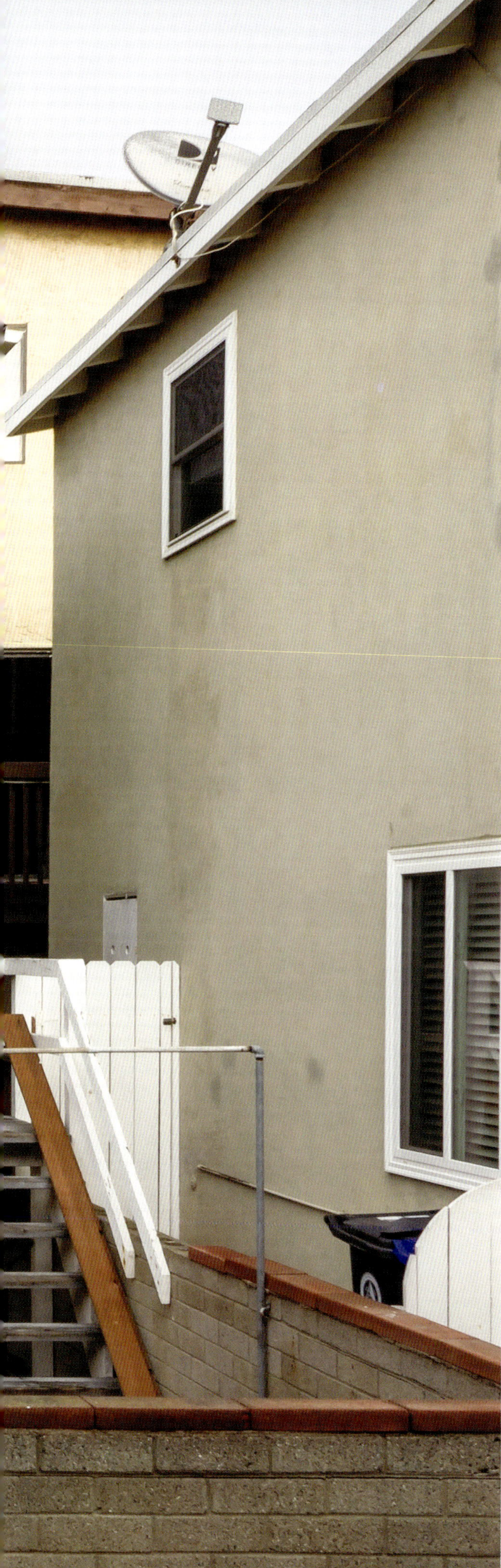

Pilgrimage

In January 2016, Gary Sweeney and his wife Janet drove a big white truck from San Antonio, Texas to his childhood home in Manhattan Beach, California. Gary is an artist who has lived in San Antonio since 1994. He was returning home to create a site-specific installation, *A Manhattan Beach Memoir: 1945-2015.* It was a pilgrimage to the place where he and his sister grew up and where his grandmother and parents lived until they died.

The truck was filled with family photos that Gary enlarged to giant, street-sign proportions and printed on rainproof MDF board, a material frequently used for commercial signage. For the installation, he covered the exterior walls of his childhood house with the photos, cutting them down to different sizes and patching them together like a puzzle. He lit the house so the images could be seen at night, each a window into another time.

After his father Mike's death in 2000 (his mother, Anita died in 1995), Gary bought his sister Gail's share of their childhood house, a 1922 beach cottage. He and his wife modernized it so they could rent it, and returned every year to visit. But because of its growing expenses and maintenance, Gary and Janet eventually decided to sell it. This would also allow Gary to retire from his full-time job as a baggage handler for 35 years.

Much has changed during the 70 years the Sweeney family lived at 320 35th Street. Manhattan Beach's middle-class neighborhood has morphed into a haven for the top 1%. The buyers planned to demolish it so they could build two townhouses covering every inch of the 30' x 90' lot, each with a potential listing price of $3 million.

"Every time a house like this disappears, it's the end of an era," said Gary. "I needed to do something to give it a proper farewell."

For the month of February 2016, Gary occupied the house, opening it up during the day and weekly at night. He took viewers on tours of the house and shared stories with old friends and neighbors. On a local level, people came by all day, every day, but the installation also received international coverage.

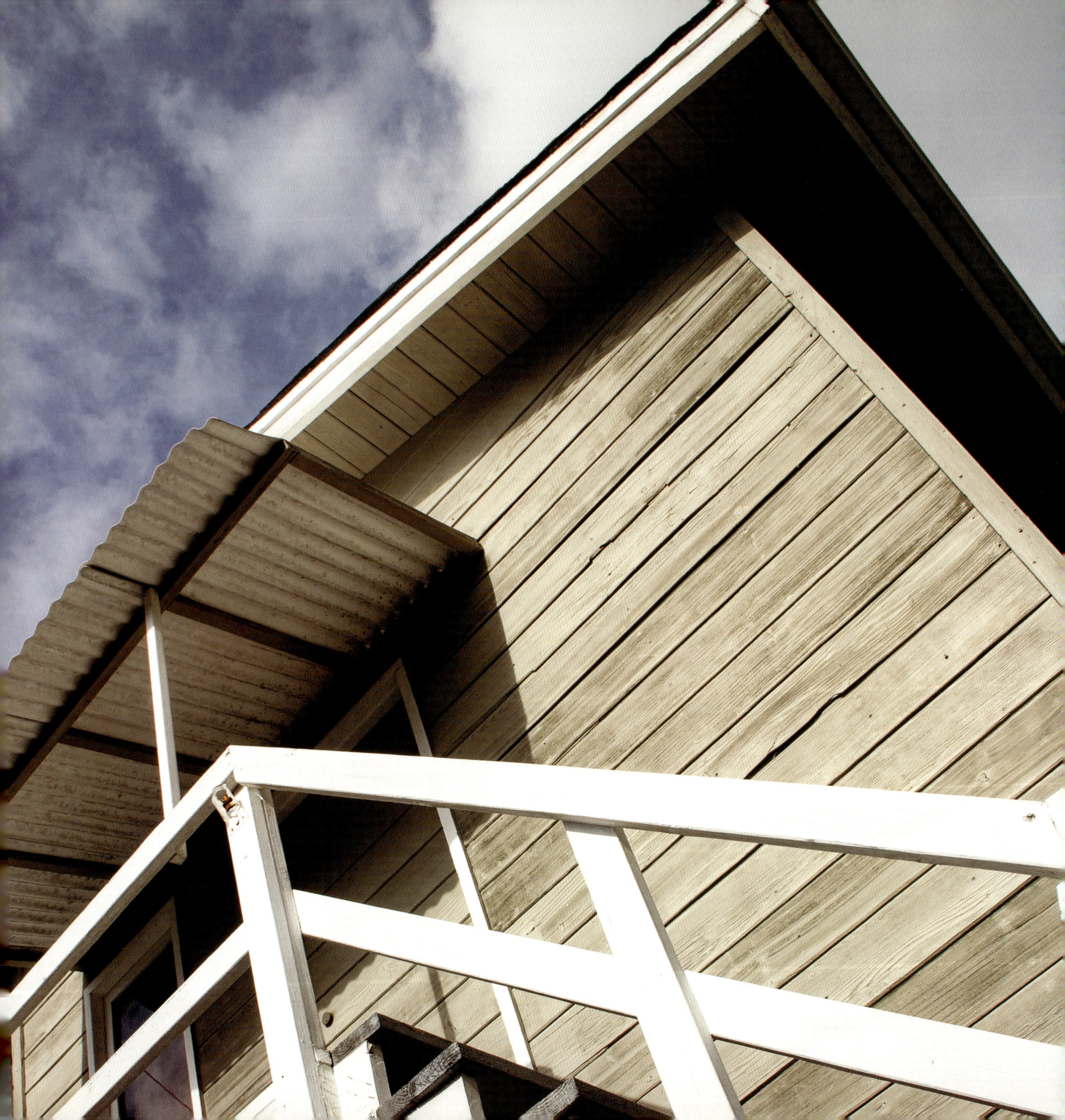

“Over 10,000 people came to see the house,” Gary recalled. One day, he came out of the shower wearing only a towel around his waist to find people in the living room (he had forgotten to lock the door). “It became a destination artwork. I had people come up and tell me they came from New York, Connecticut, Michigan, Tennessee, Washington, and Idaho—just to see the project.”

“The installation caught on like wildfire. My high school had a reunion there, there was an opening party, a closing party, and parties in between. My friends came up with excuses to have events there; the whole South Bay community got together and embraced it. It was the best possible send-off I could get.”

While the project was simple and straightforward—an artist’s goodbye to his childhood home—Gary’s use of photography, the site-specific nature of the installation, and the personal subject matter made it more than an exercise in nostalgia. His installation was a clever riff on family history using elements of West Coast Pop. Traditional Pop art took on the conventions of mass media and advertising, making popular culture its subject. Gary applies Pop techniques to other subjects: personal origin, family, and relationships.

In the age of the Internet, his use of old photographs resonates with the many changes that have happened since photography turned digital. One of the biggest changes is the way in which photography gets distributed. The cumbersome process of developing paper prints from negatives is no longer necessary. Images may be replicated and broadcast around the world with the touch of a button. Because of social media, we’re accustomed to seeing personal subject matter everywhere. But when Gary returns these private images to the real world, it jolts viewers from the present into the past.

Most family photos get displayed on desks and side tables, on bulletin boards and refrigerators, but Gary’s are downloaded on the street where he grew up. In an era of oversharing, that’s not such an unusual move, but Gary celebrates his parents in the real, not the virtual, world—the pictures of his parents are not posted on Facebook but on his home, to be seen by a neighborhood, not a network.

"One night during the installation, while I was living in the house, I had already turned out the lights but my wife heard voices. There were three people outside in the street looking around. I decided to turn on the lights, and it ended up being the Monseigneur from the American Martyrs Church, the Catholic church we attended. I was an altar boy. He was the one who gave my father's eulogy. I brought him and his two assistants in and gave them the tour. We talked for two hours."

Gary maintains an active online presence, but his installation is a retro move that goes full circle, a re-appreciation of the past, like the return of the LP or favoring hand-scripted letters over text. The photos that he affixed to his home are a clever foil to the digital age: a radical sharing of an analog archive. This is not the first radical sharing he has done: since 1990, he has sent 35,000 postcards to friends and family. He alters and collages them so that they become a form of mail art. In 2010, they became the subject of his limited-edition book, *Post Obsessive.*

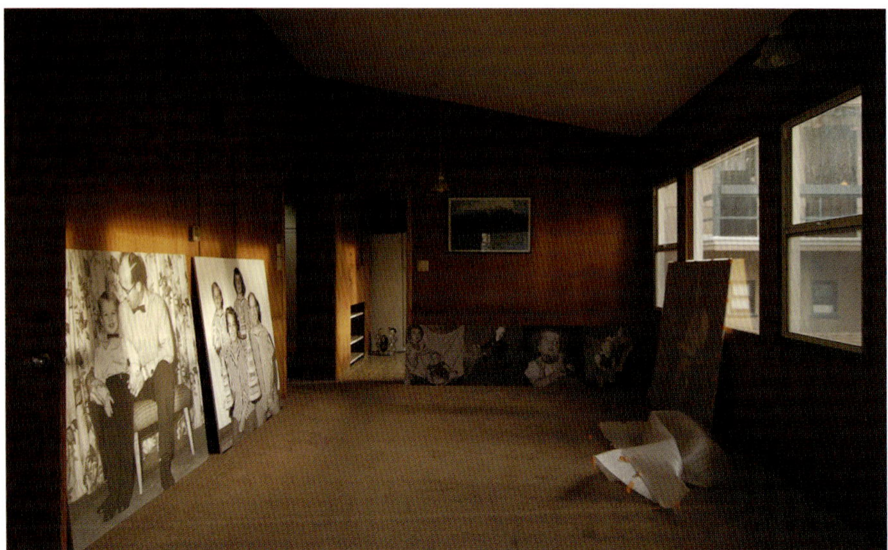

ABOVE » The empty house was used in its last days as a staging area for the installation.

RIGHT » Backyard installation views of *Manhattan Beach Memoir,* 2016

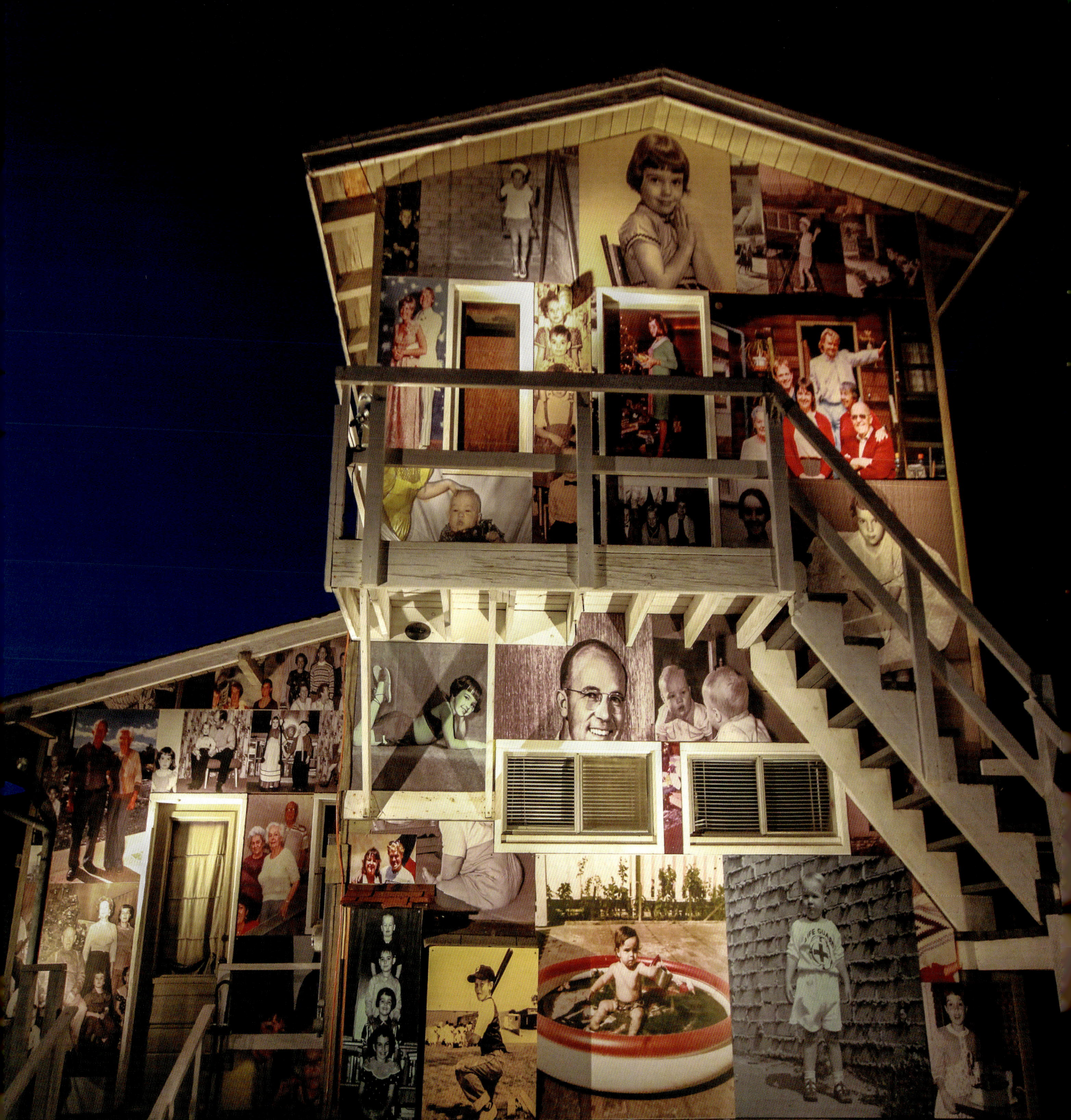

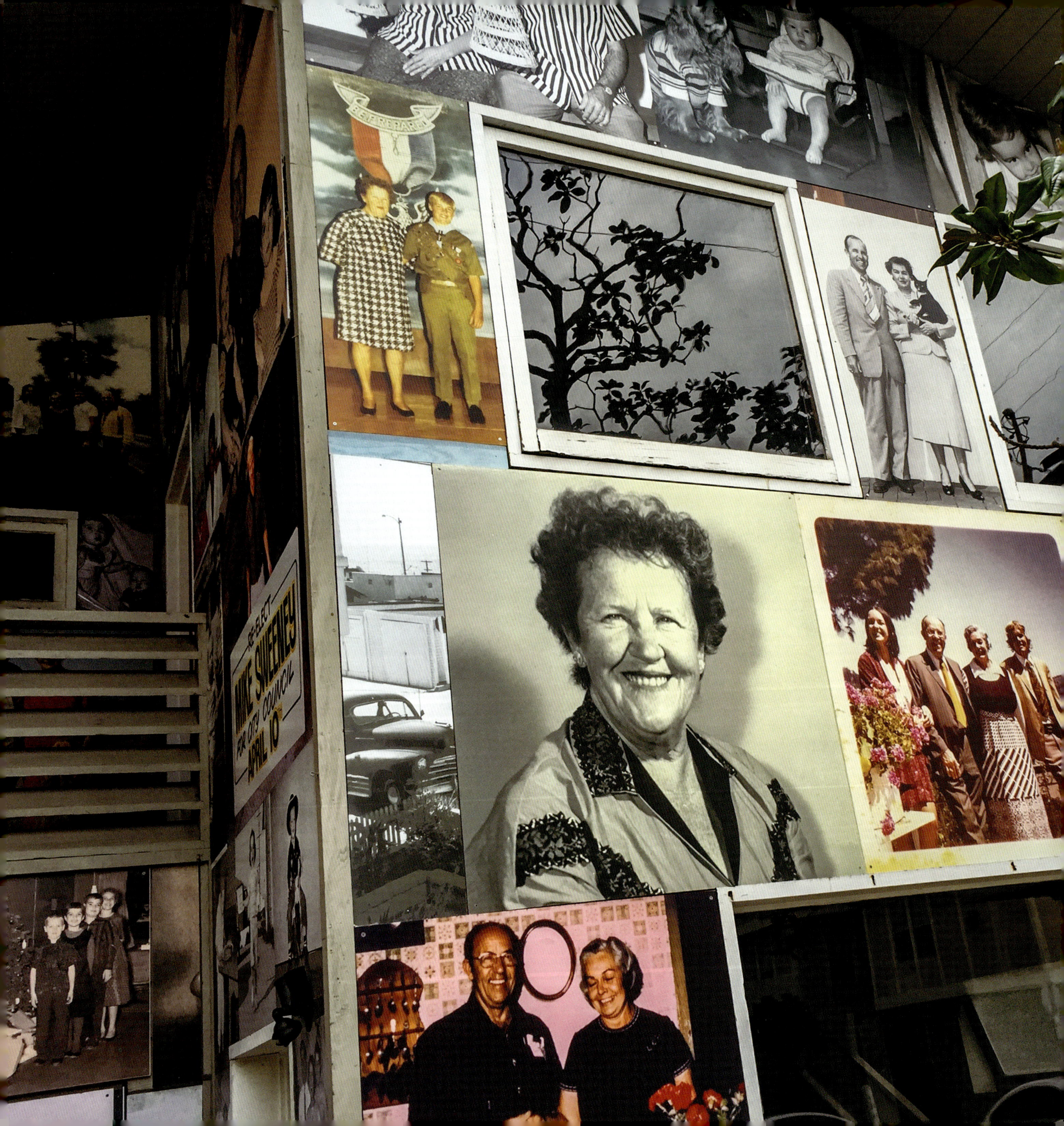
BE PREPARED
RE-ELECT
MIKE SWEENEY
FOR CITY COUNCIL
APRIL 10TH

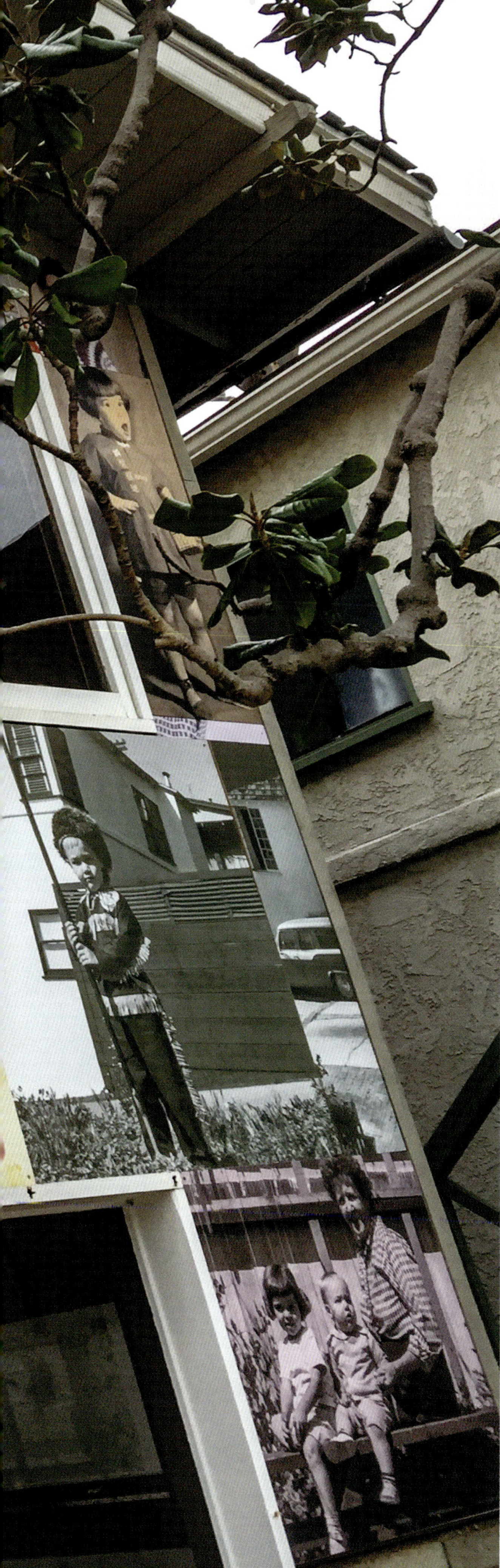

The House

A house is like a pictorial frame delimiting the lives lived within it. Gary's *Manhattan Beach Memoir* is an homage to this frame, this sheltered space, made resonant by the role it played in his family's life.

"Walking through the house to get to the backside, [Gary] stopped and pointed to a square outline on the living room wall where a clock hung for decades. 'I bet I've looked up at that blank space 10 times to check what time it is,' he said. 'It's just instinctive.'" [1]

Houses contain the act of living: worn paint on the face of a frequently opened cabinet, a rough spot on the flooring by the door, traffic patterns across the carpet. Physical patterns in the external world echo our different forms of memories. Implicit memories are habits and skills. Explicit memories are what we're conscious of, what we're trying to remember. Old photographs transcend these boundaries; careful studies of the photos may reinforce the explicit while revealing the implicit. The images play tricks with our awareness—what registers with us one year may disappear into the background the next year, like the ever-widening scope of perception in the developmental spectrum of a child. Falling into life's comfortable groove mimics the way we form memories, returning again and again to certain pathways laid down long ago.

Manhattan Beach Memoir is a celebration not just of a bygone era, a family's life, but of a particular landscape and a use of photography that is also disappearing into the past. As his humble beach cottage gets replaced by townhomes and the city succumbs to an ever-growing homogeneous suburbia, Gary's art performs a similar function to the landscape photography of Walker Evans: "Without Walker Evans to remind them of how things once were, swaths of America would not know that there was more to their ancestral world than Bed Bath & Beyond," Geoff Dyer observed. [2]

LEFT » Front installation view of *Manhattan Beach Memoir* featuring an image of Maggie Sweeney (black and white) shown above her studio apartment.

Meanwhile, with digital photography, the organizing of images becomes fractured into faces and places. Images stay suspended in the cloud. Without the physical existences of negatives and albums, the holistic record of a family is shattered into the various hard drives and cloud accounts. The camera lens has become integrated into every moment of the day; turned inwards, like the mind's eye. This increased accessibility allows for another type of photography that can be intimate and banal, like visual note taking. This compounding multiplicity of images fills more of the in-between spaces, cheapening and desensitizing the recording of time.

Through his installation at his childhood house, Gary was able to return once more and see it through the lens of his father's camera, and through the artist he became, in contrast to the child who lived there.

The documentary *The Cool School* ends with a quote by Walter Hopps that best describes what Gary did when he shared his family memories with not only his neighborhood but the world: "Art offers the possibility of love with strangers," he said, quoting a poet friend of his. "They think they have to interpret it, but all you have to do is see it. But you have to put a lot of baggage aside to see it." [3]

RIGHT » Front porch installation detail

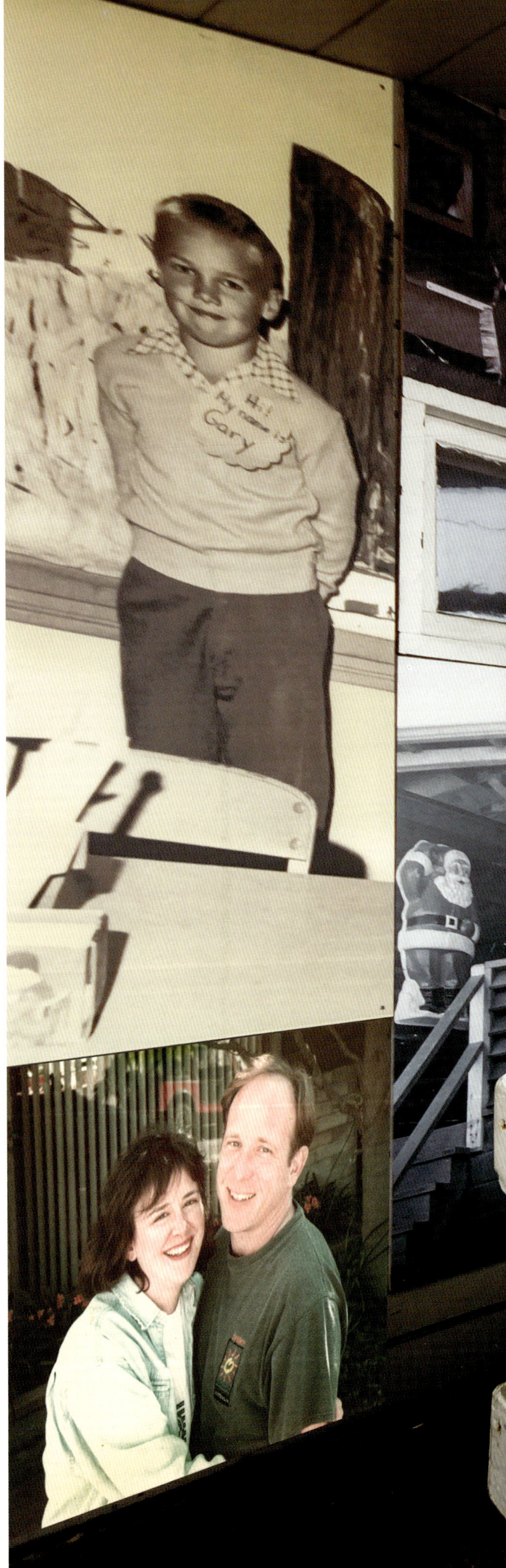

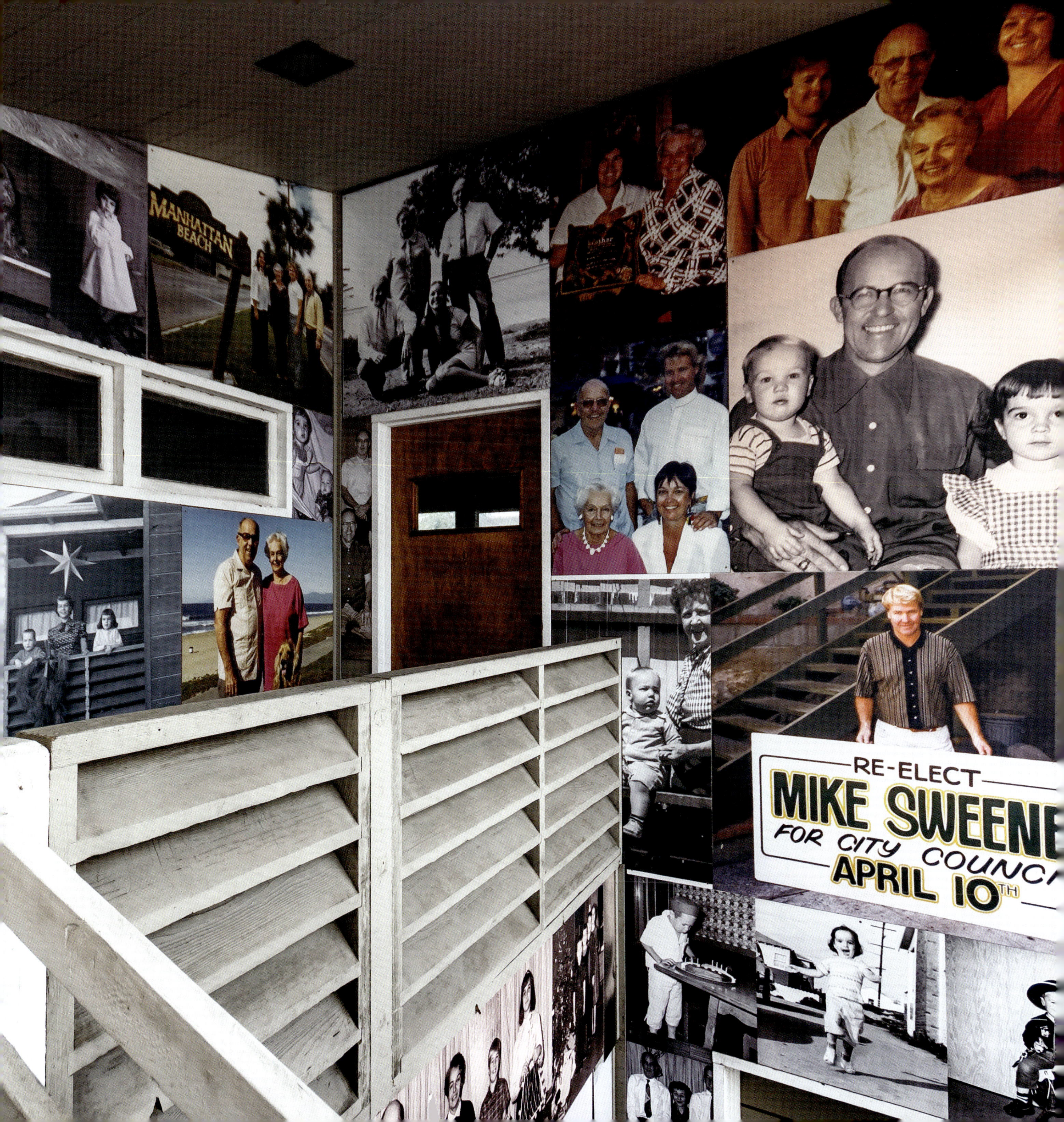
MANHATTAN
BEACH
RE-ELECT
MIKE SWEENE
FOR CITY COUNC
APRIL 10TH

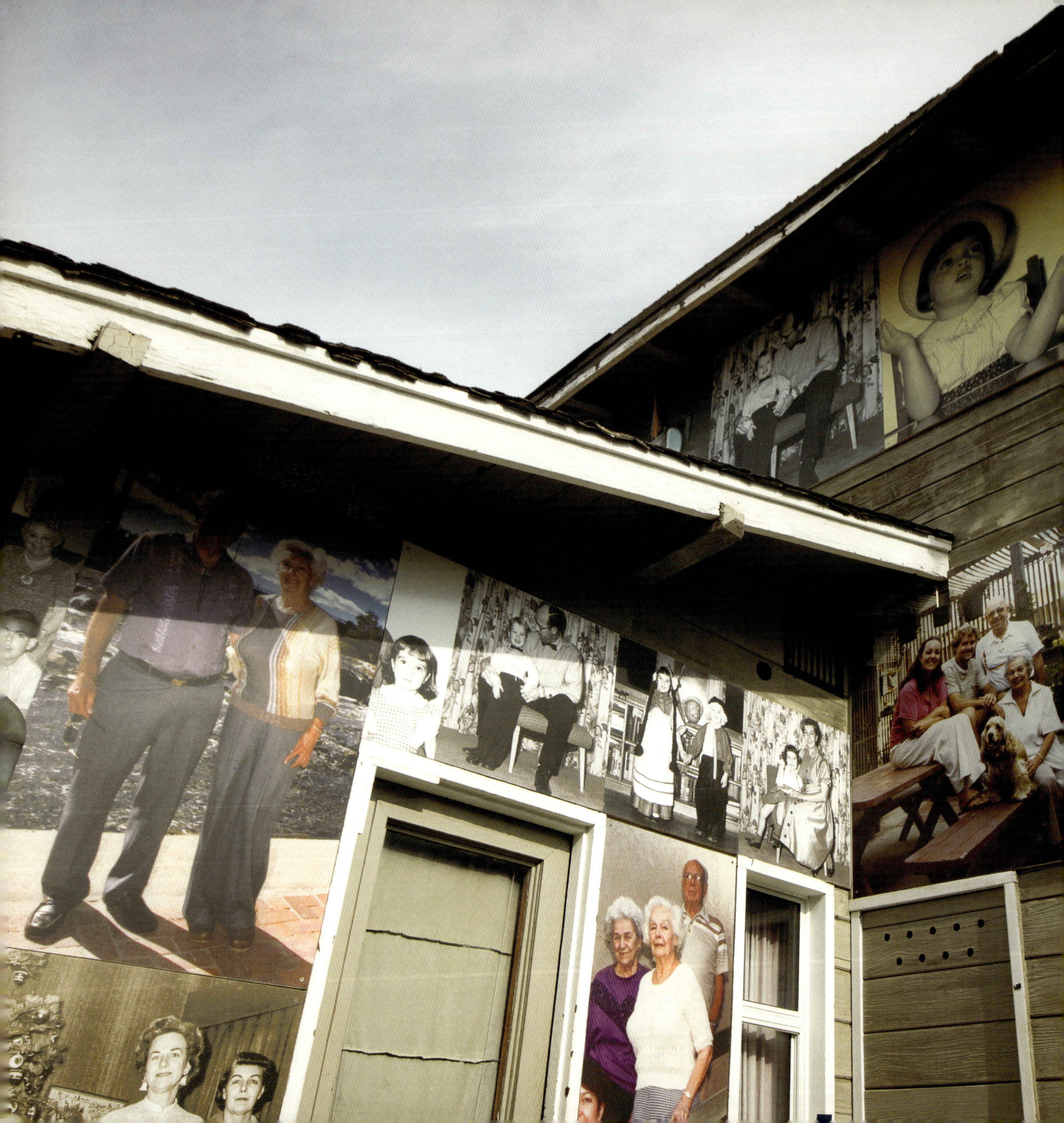

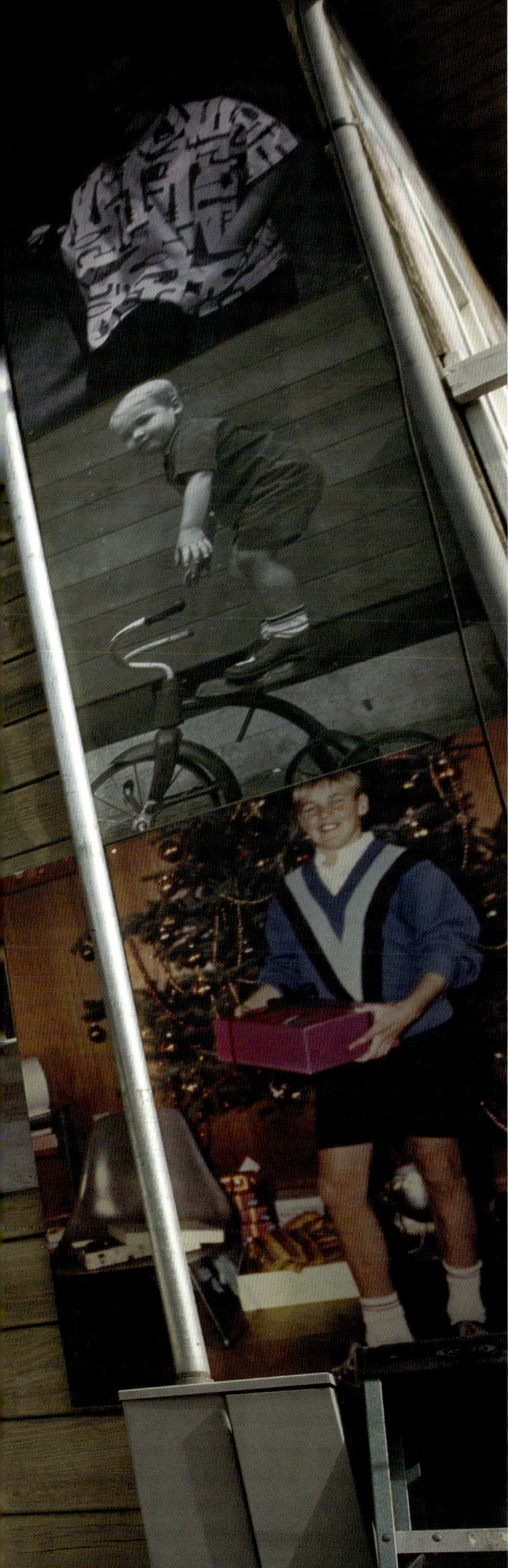

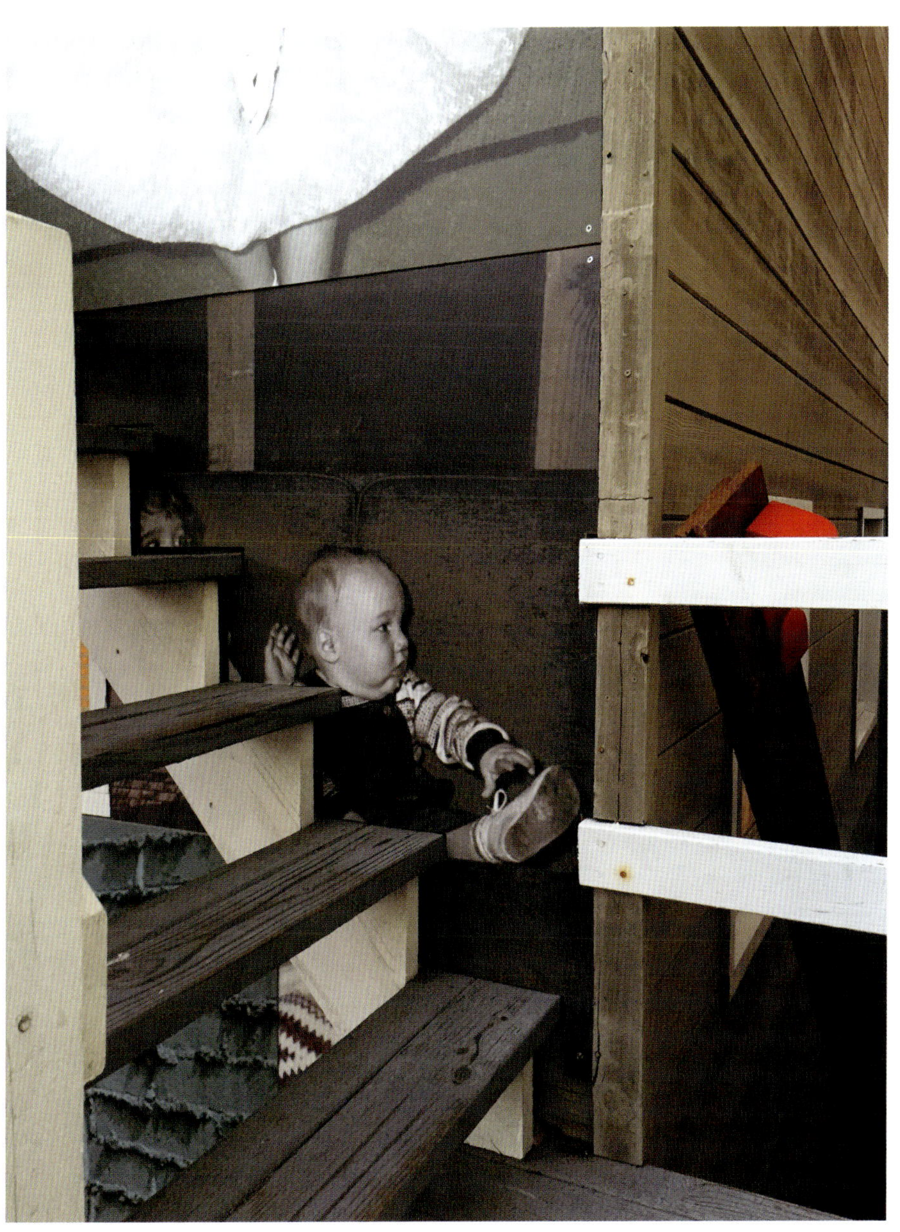

LEFT / ABOVE / FOLLOWING » Back porch installation details

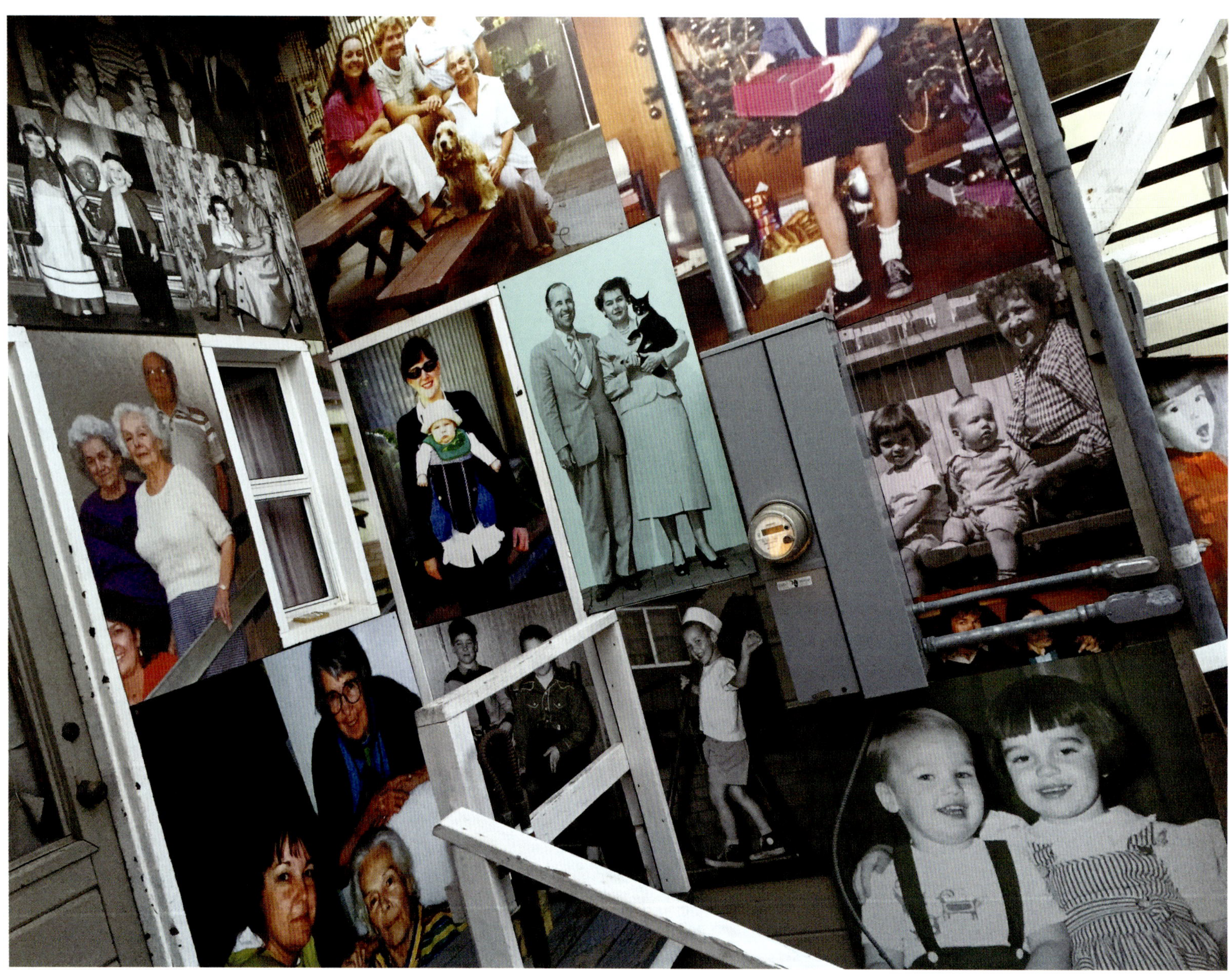

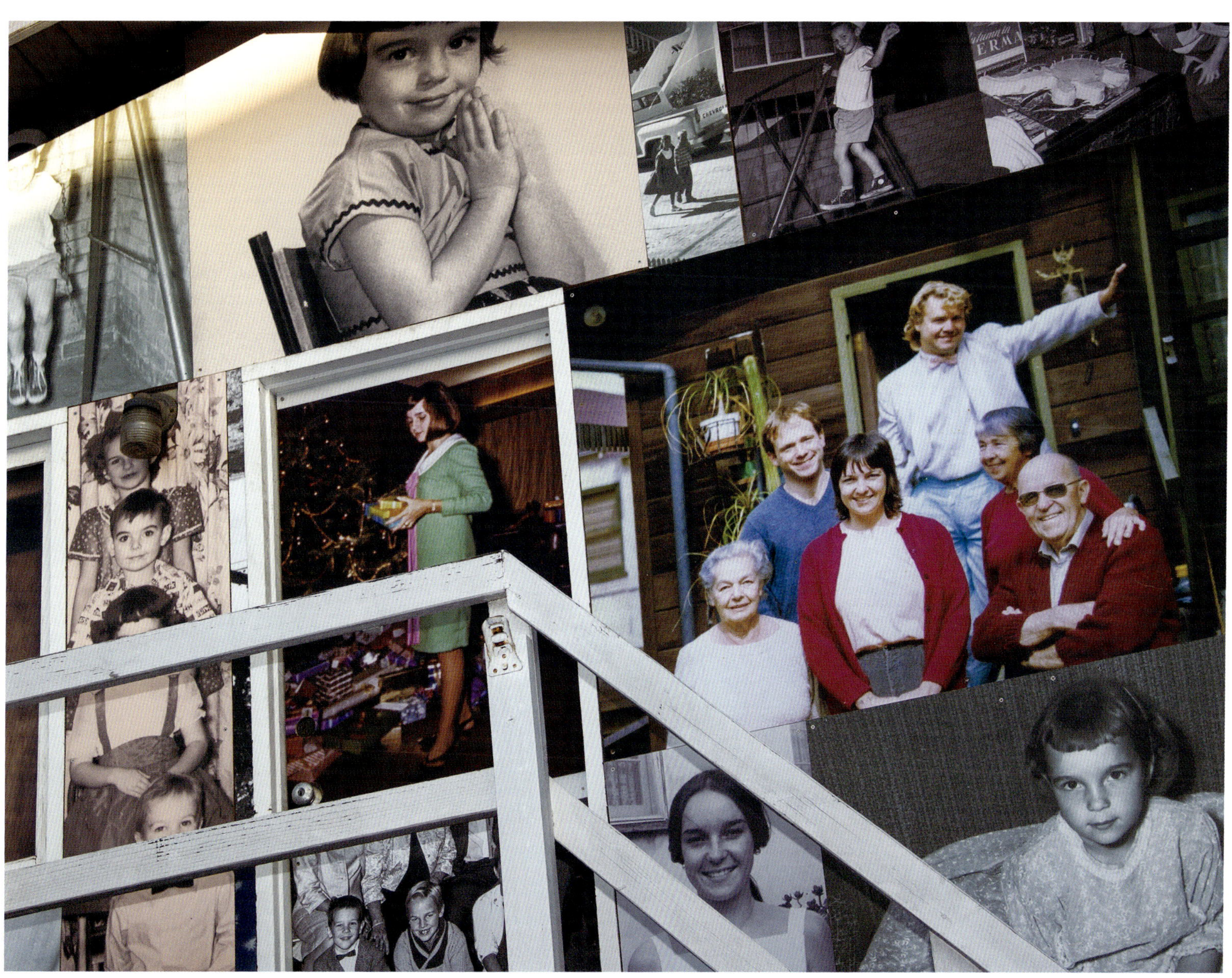

Origin Story

Manhattan Beach is part of a larger area called South Bay, named because of its location along the southern shore of Santa Monica Bay. South Bay includes 15 cities and parts of southwest Los Angeles. Before Manhattan Beach was a city in southwestern Los Angeles County, there were only miles and miles of sand dunes, dotted with purple wild verbena and scrub brush, sacred spaces marked by indigenous trails and burial grounds.[4] In 1837, the area, including ten miles of Pacific coastline, was part of an almost 25,000-acre Mexican land grant that was given to Antonio Ygnacio Avila (1781-1858); it became *Rancho Sausal Redondo* (Round Willow Grove Ranch).

In 1868, the Avila family sold the ranch to a Scotsman, Sir Robert Burnett, who used the land to raise sheep and cattle. Burnett moved back to Scotland and leased the land to Daniel Freeman, who ranched and planted almond, olive, and citrus groves. During the 1875 drought, Freeman turned to dry farming the land.

In 1895, a former plantation owner, Colonel Blanton Duncan from Virginia, bought the Manhattan Beach area of land for $1,000 in gold coin and built one of the first houses and piers.

In 1902, two developers flipped a coin on who got to name their prospective beach suburb. The winner, Stewart Merrill, named it "Manhattan" after his original home on the East Coast.

During the 1920-30s, Hollywood movie studios filmed desert scenes on the north side of Manhattan Beach. When the sand became a nuisance, encroaching on streets, boardwalks, and light posts, the 50' to 70' high dunes were leveled. The excess amount of pristine, white sand was sold to develop Hawaii's Waikiki Beach.

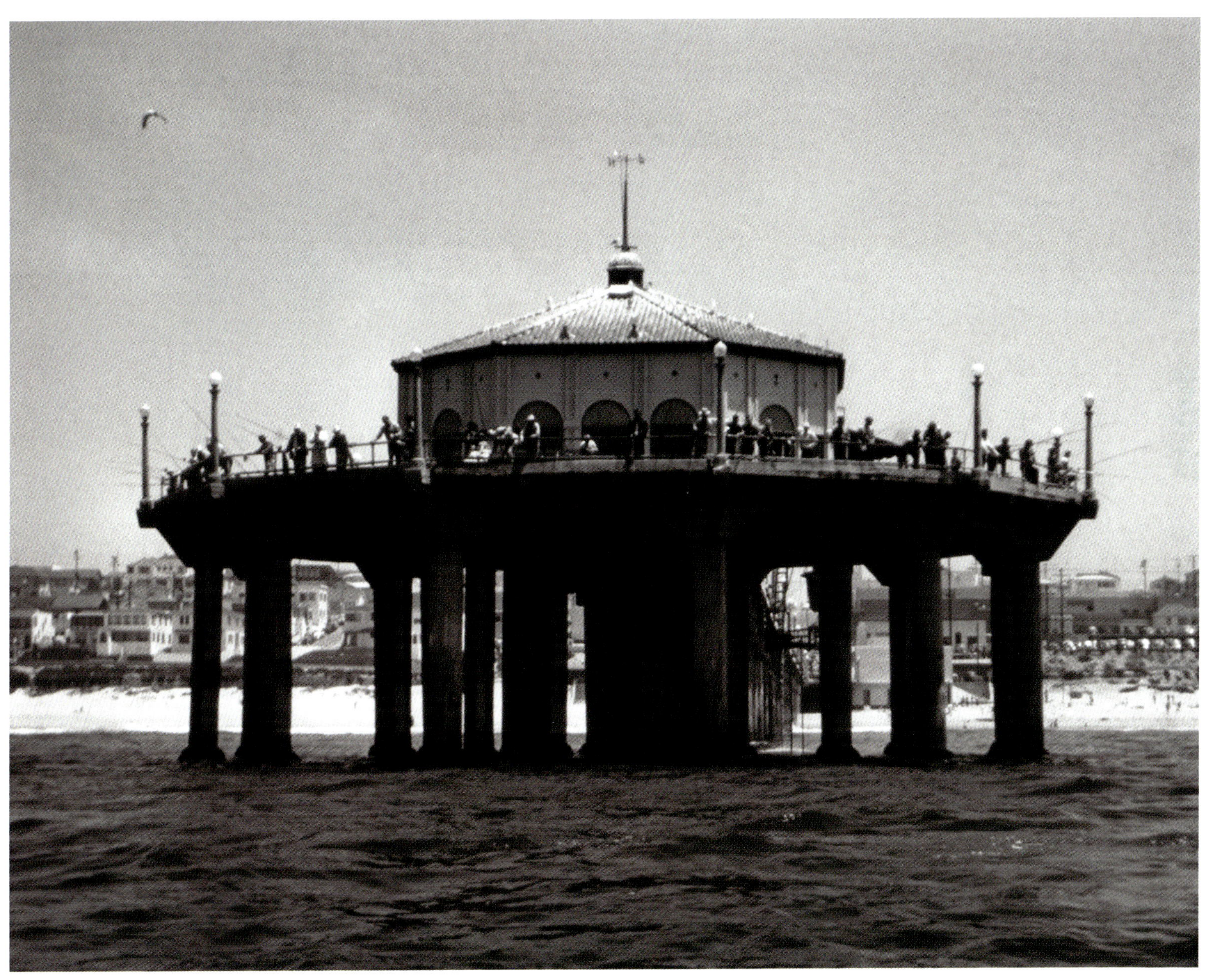

» Manhattan Beach Pier, built in 1920

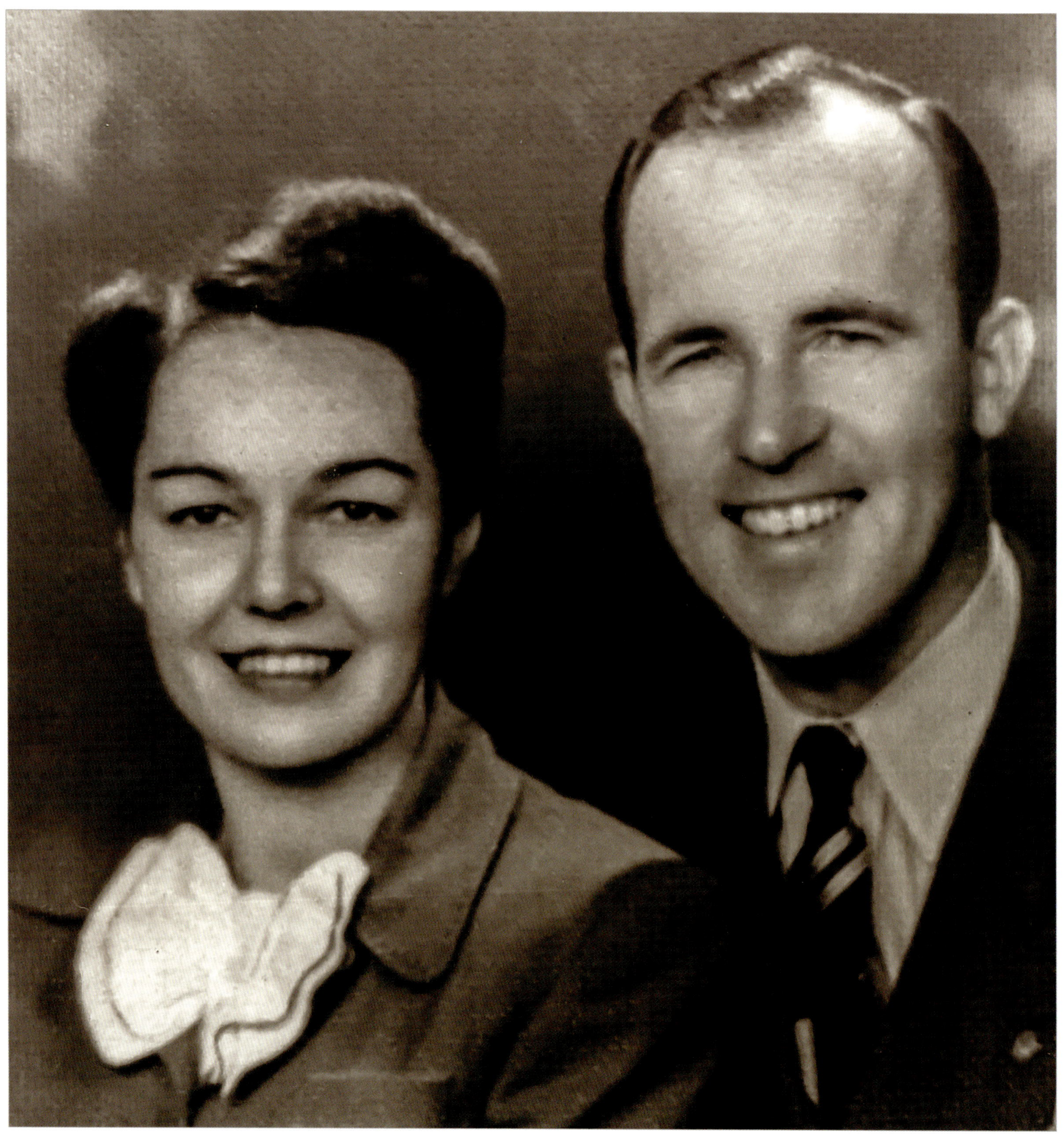

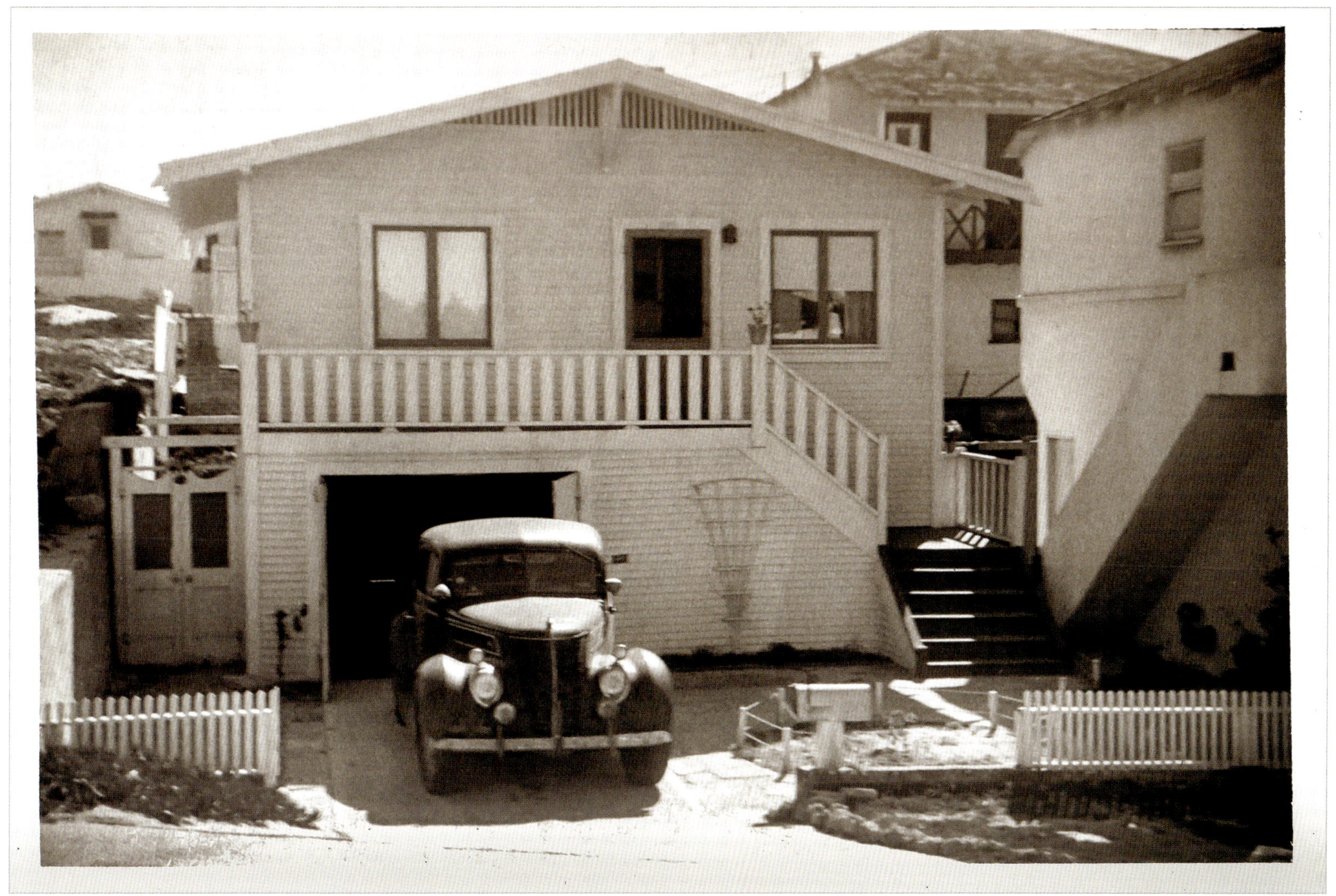

LEFT » Mike Sweeney and Anita Felsing were married on April 5, 1942

ABOVE » 320 35th Street, Manhattan Beach, 1945

Anita bought the Sweeney's small beach cottage completely furnished in 1945 while her husband, Mike, was still serving in the Pacific during WWII. When Mike moved home, he customized the house to accommodate his family, building a wide, easily accessible set of stairs along the side for Anita, who had contracted polio while she trained as a nursing student. In the 1950s, Mike and the neighbors jacked up the house, in the Amish tradition, and built an apartment and garage on the downstairs level for his mother, Maggie, to come and live in. At the same time, he added a darkroom to the top of the house.

"It was a man cave before there were man caves," said Gary. The stairs leading up to it were ship ladder style, only accessible from the exterior. Because of her physical limitations resulting from polio, his mother never saw the inside of the darkroom.

RIGHT » Gary and his sister Gail in the backyard addition built in 1954. Downstairs was Gary's bedroom and upstairs was built as a darkroom for Mike's photography.

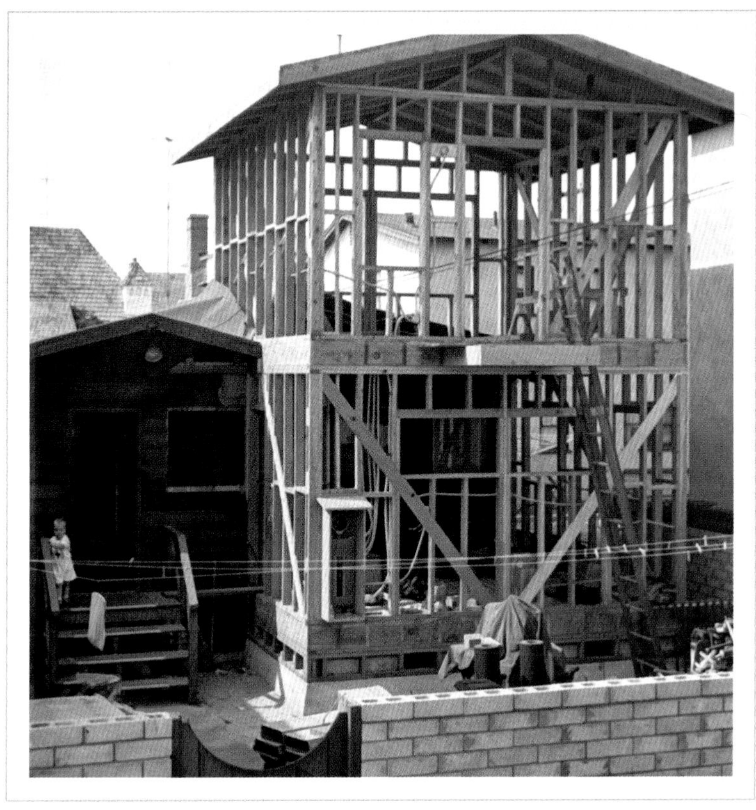
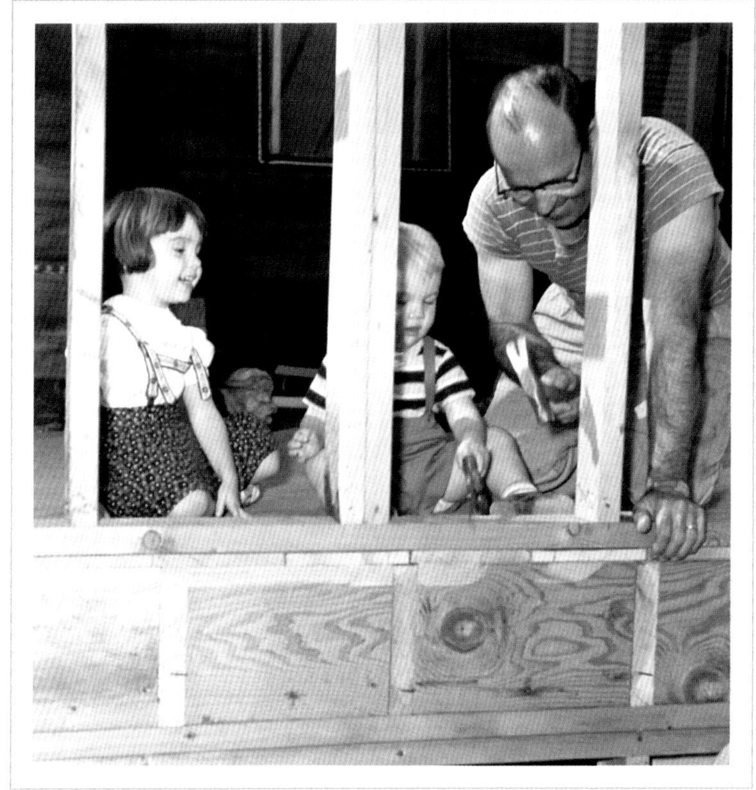
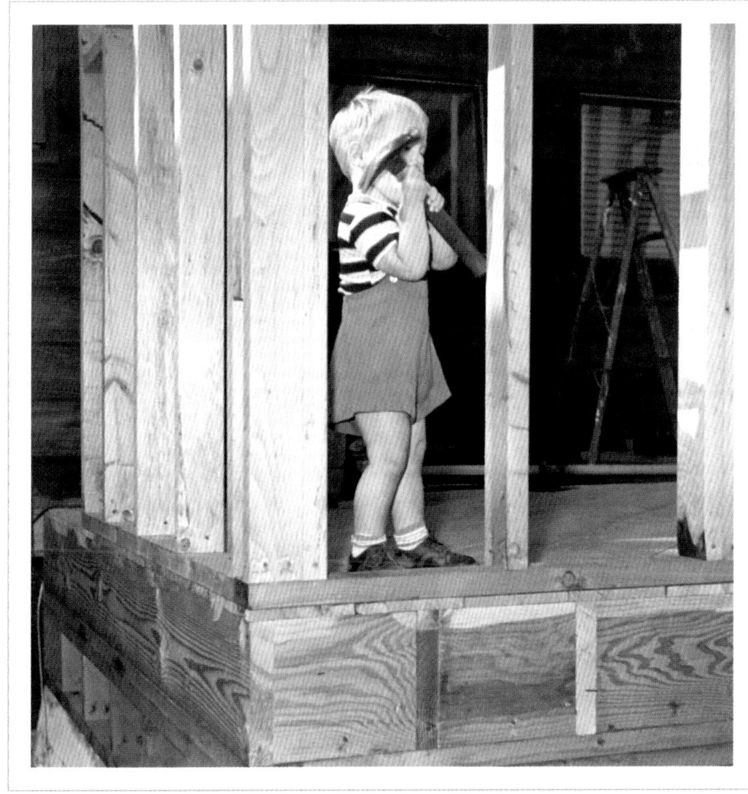
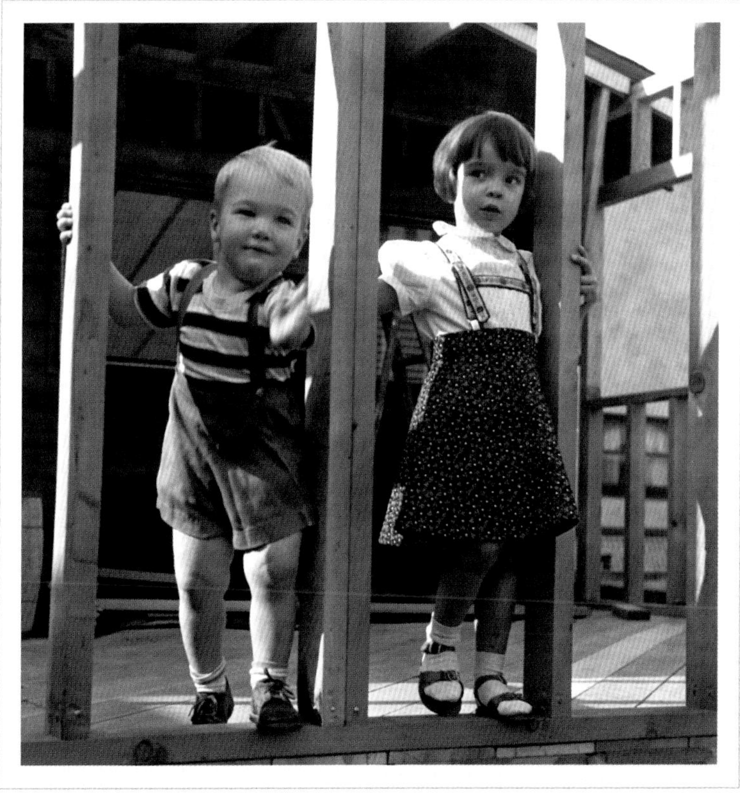

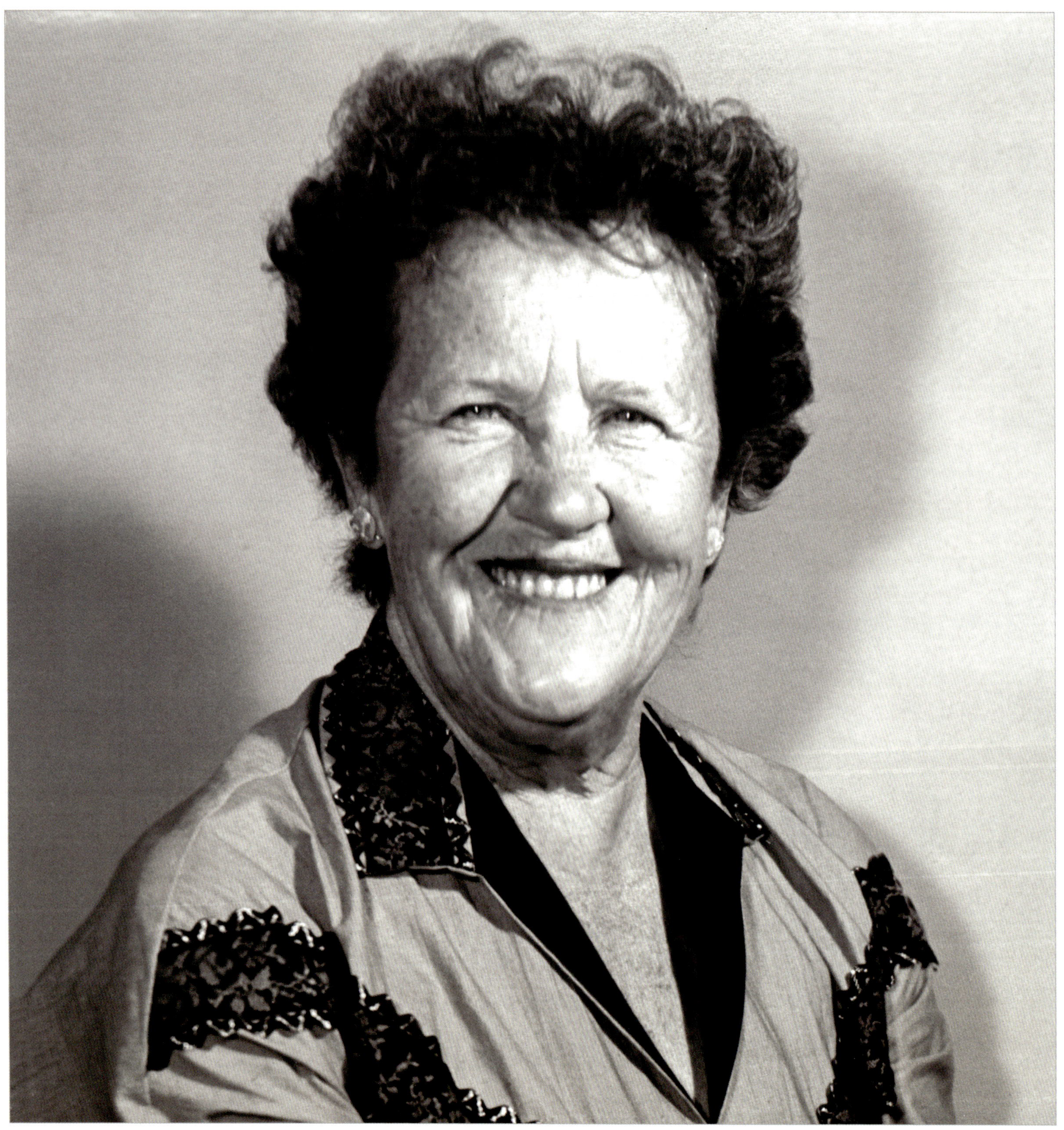

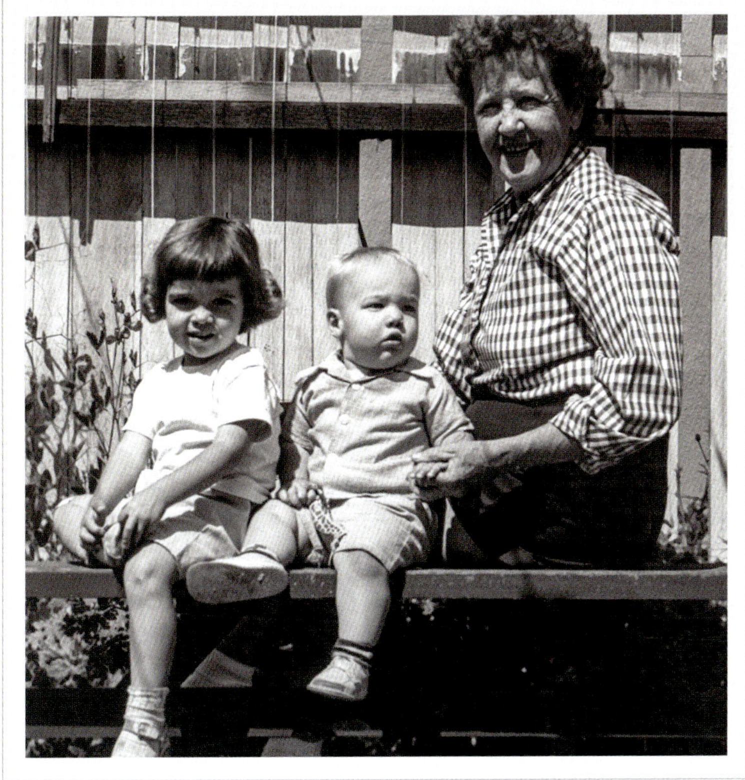

Maggie Sweeney

Margaret ("Maggie") Sweeney, my paternal grandmother, lived in the downstairs apartment of our house from 1960 until her death, in 1973. A single mother of two children, she drove her mother and my young father and his sister from Oklahoma to Los Angeles to escape the Dust Bowl of the 1930s.

The influence she had on my artistic sensibility cannot be overstated. Her apartment was filled with art books, modernist furniture, and her own paintings. Her sense of style and taste carried through every aspect of her life, and I'm grateful that she lived long enough to embarrass me at my first solo exhibit in 1973:

> *"Do you see these artworks? My GRANDSON made ALL OF THESE! Aren't they AMAZING?"*

» While Maggie was very much a part of everyday life in the Sweeney household, she was a matriarch with an independent life and identity. She hosted salons in the '50s and invited architects and playwrights to her downstairs apartment and was the inspiration for a character in one of her friends' plays.

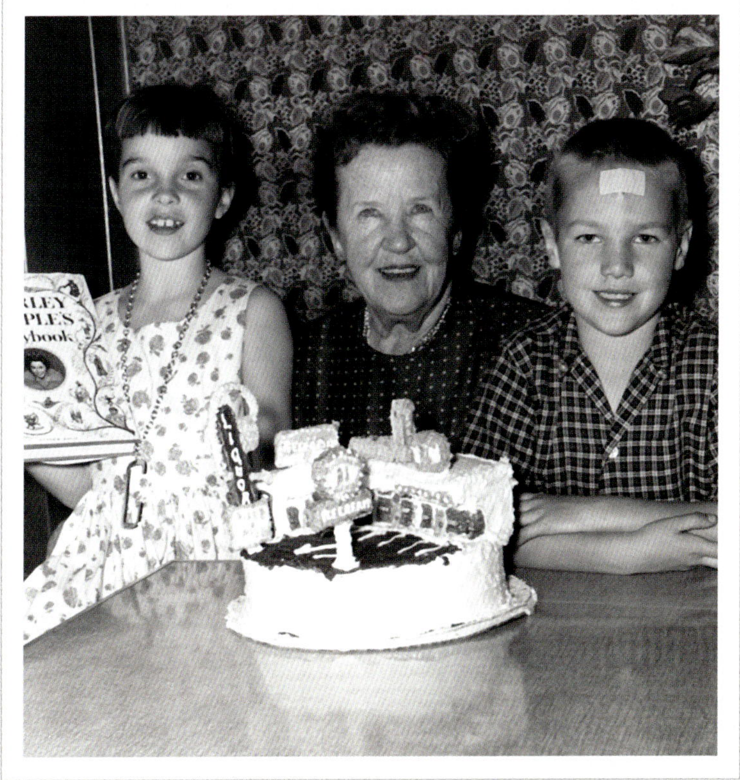

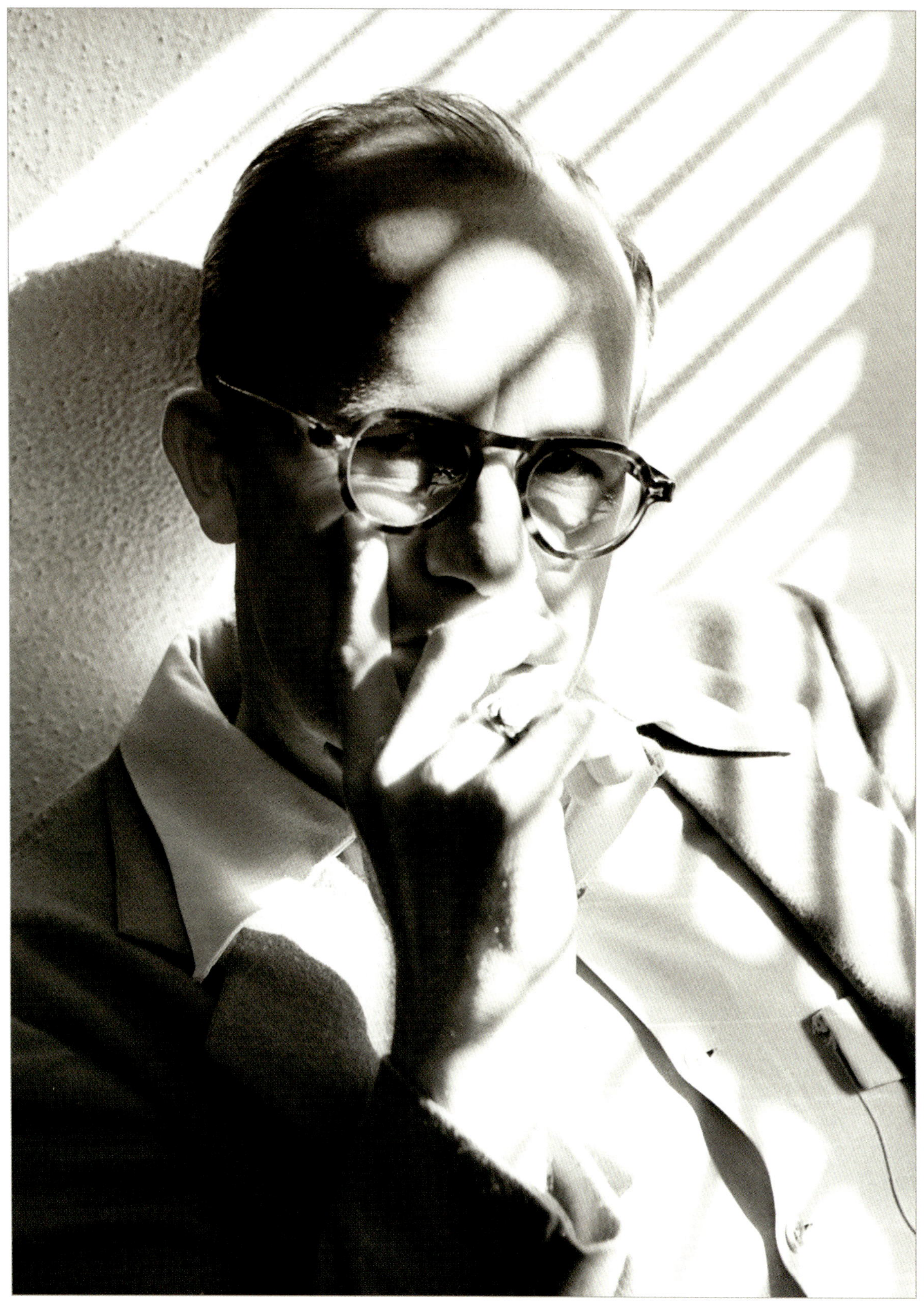

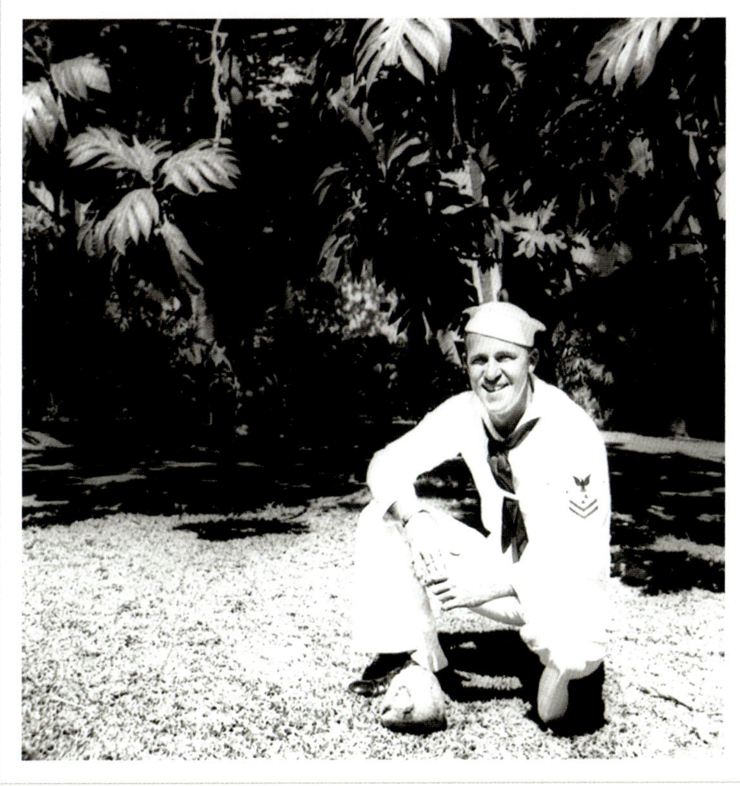

Mike Sweeney

Mike Sweeney, my father, was born in McAllister, Oklahoma, in 1916. Like many people during the Depression, he found work where he could while attending school, notably at the boat house in MacArthur Park, and later at a garage in Hollywood. He joined the Navy at the start of World War II, and was part of the famed "SeaBees" unit on Guam. He came home to the new house in Manhattan Beach and joined the Los Angeles Police Department, rising to the rank of Detective Sergeant. After retiring, he opened Sweeney's Hardware in Manhattan Beach, a local family-run institution that operated until 1988. During his time in Manhattan Beach, Mike was active in the PTA, Cub Scouts, The Chamber of Commerce, The South Bay Water District, and the Coordinating Council. He was a city councilman for twenty years, and mayor three times. He was awarded the "Rose and Scroll" Citizen of the Year, the only recipient to have been awarded the honor twice. After an extended illness, my father died in the house on December 29, 2000.

» Many photographers are often absent within their own photo libraries—present only as the lens rather than the subject. However, Mike's thoughtful staging techniques and shutter release equipment allowed him to be present in the family album as both photographer and subject.

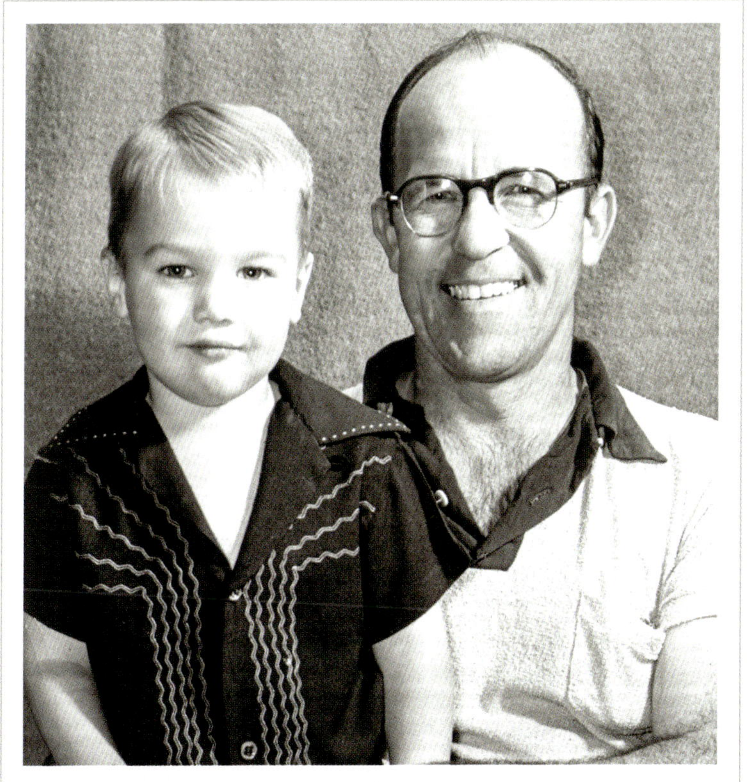

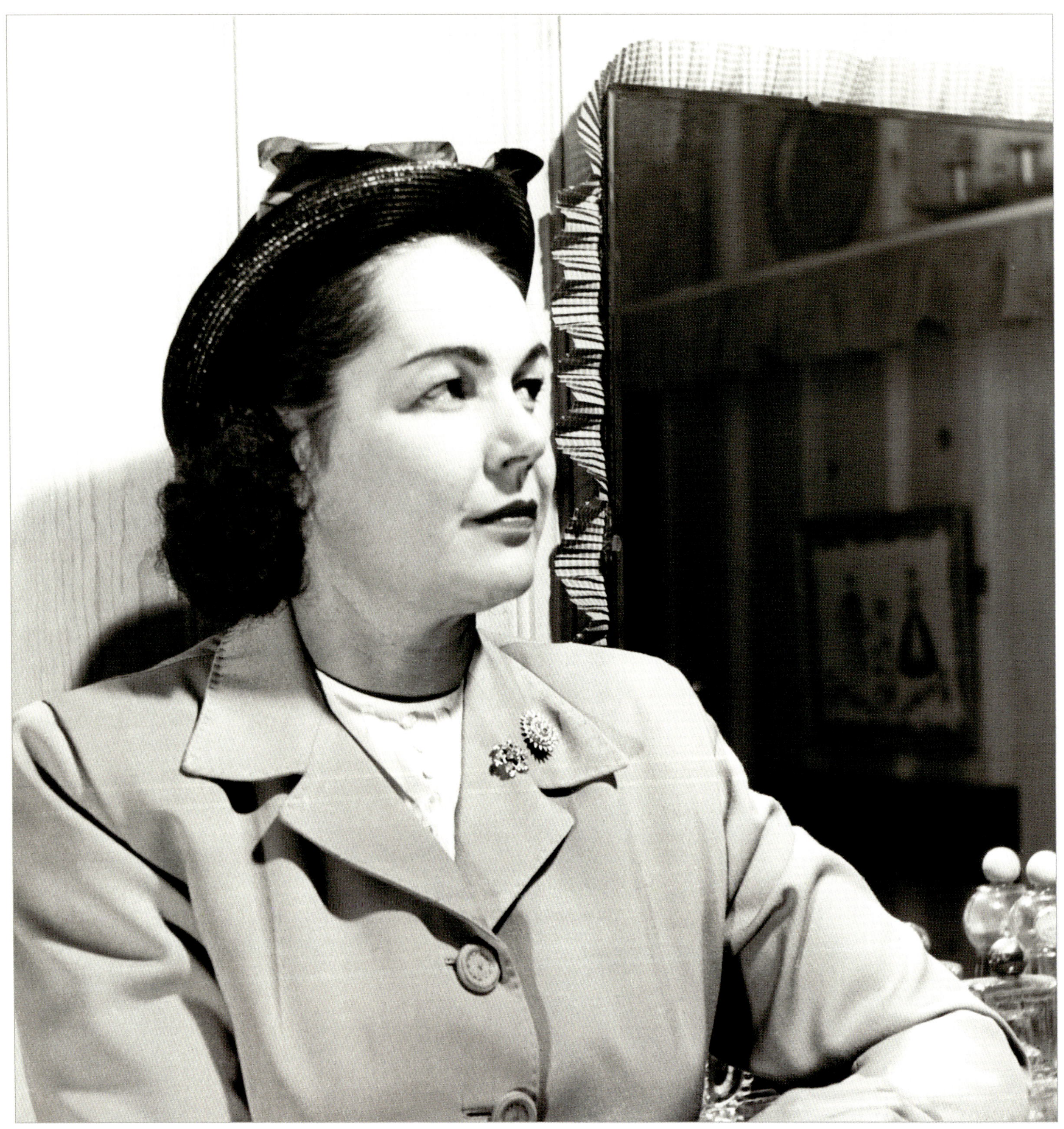

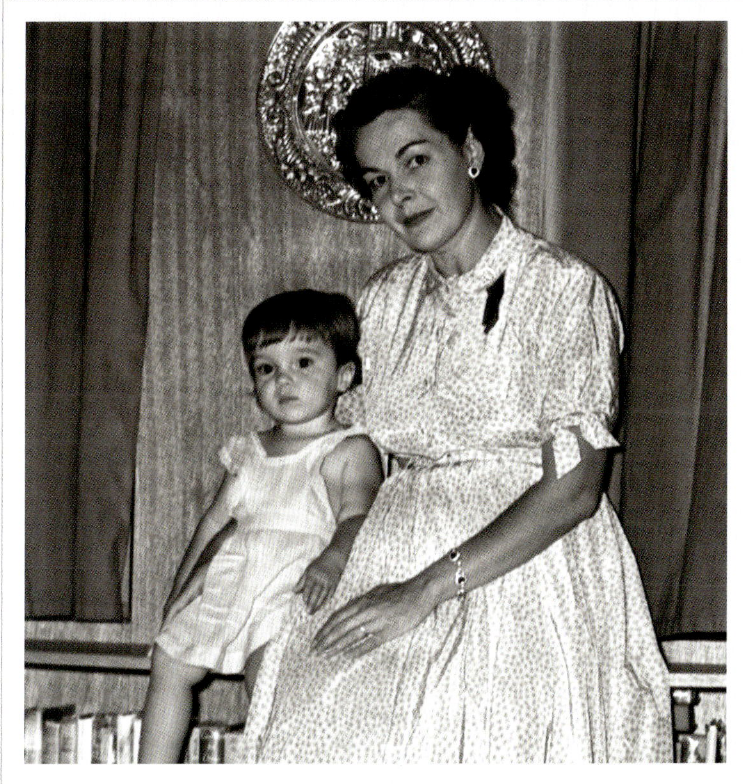

Anita Sweeney

Anita Felsing, my mother, was the youngest of William and Margaret Felsing's three children. She was born in 1915 and raised in Los Angeles where she attended nursing school during the polio epidemic of the 1930s. While there, her class was assigned to work at the hospital and massage the legs of polio victims. She and her entire class fell victim to the disease, and it affected her mobility for the rest of her life. She purchased the Manhattan Beach house in 1945 and lived there until her death in 1995.

» *In the early '50s when we were young, the camera was out all the time.*

Anita Sweeney was a loving stay-at-home mom with many creative interests. She had a greenhouse in the backyard and was an award-winning orchid grower. She was also a member of the Orchid Society of Southern California. In addition to creating expressive flower arrangements, Anita also made enamel and copper jewelry in collaboration with her husband, Mike.

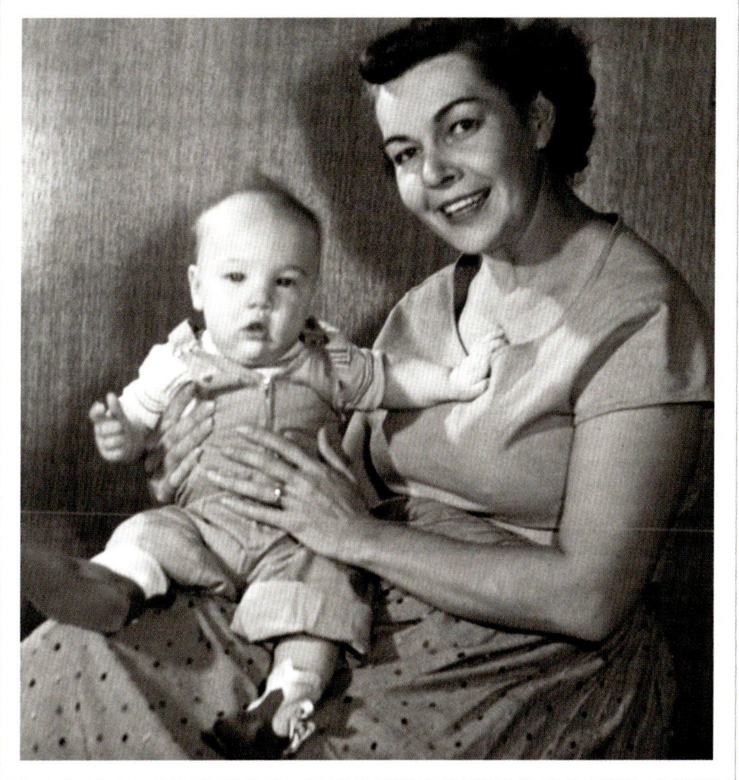

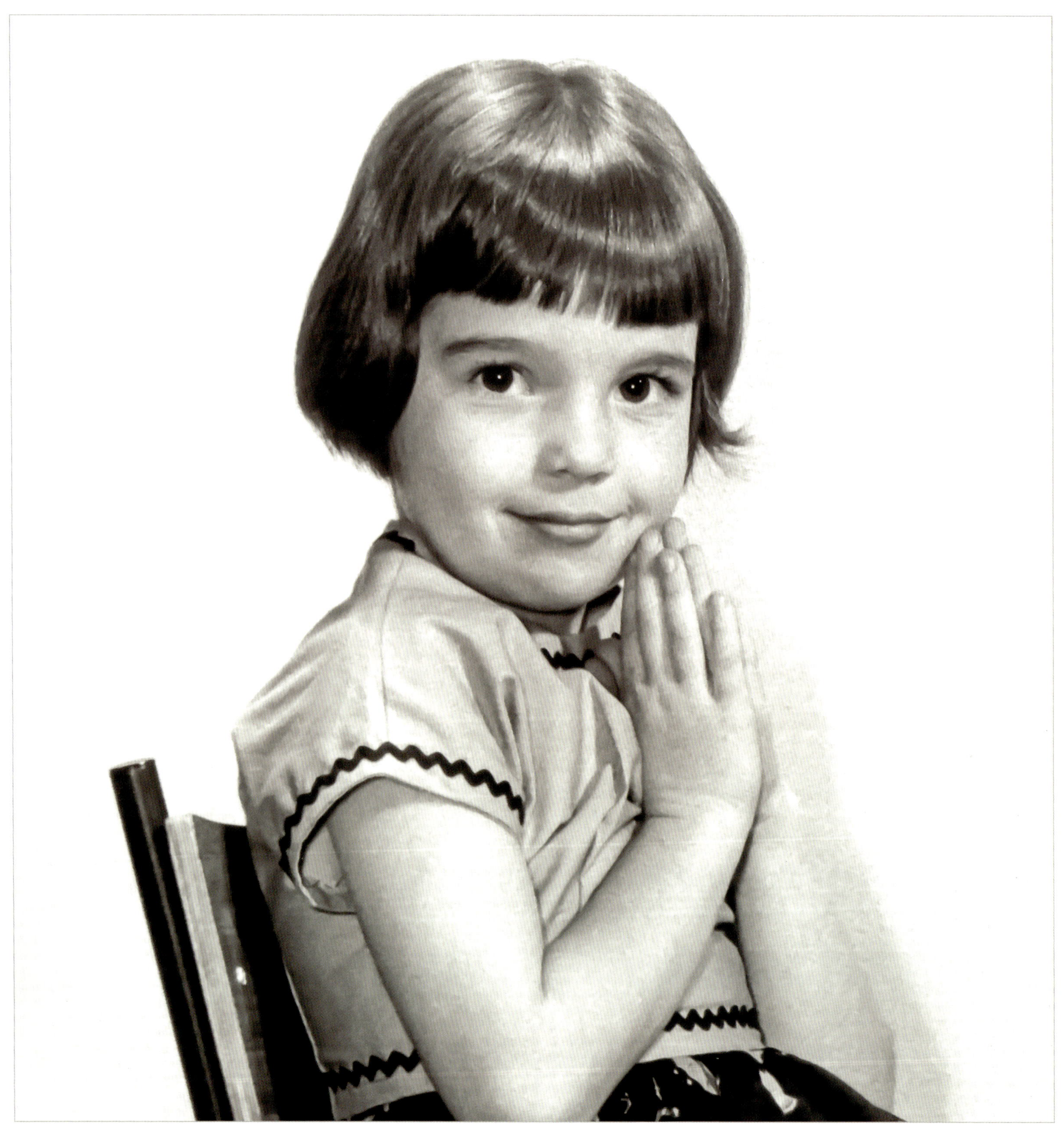

Gail Sweeney

Gail Sweeney, my sister, was born March 5, 1951. Because so many of the neighborhood kids were her age, I was "Gail's little brother" for most of my school years. She graduated with a degree in History from College of the Redwoods in Humboldt County, and spent much of her adult life working as a book seller in Pacific Grove, next to Monterey. She moved back to Manhattan Beach to take care of our father during the last years of his life, and now divides her time between California and her home in Italy.

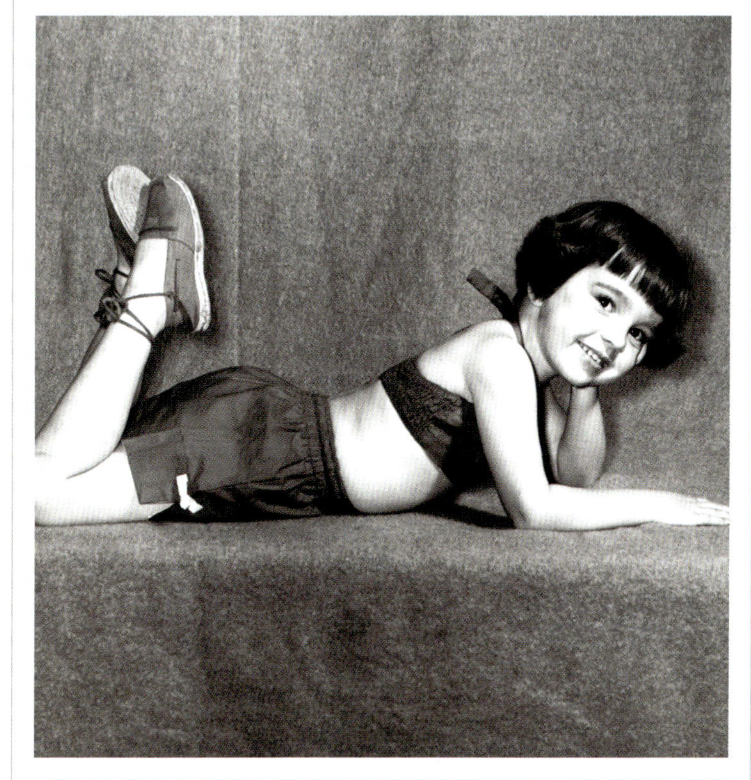

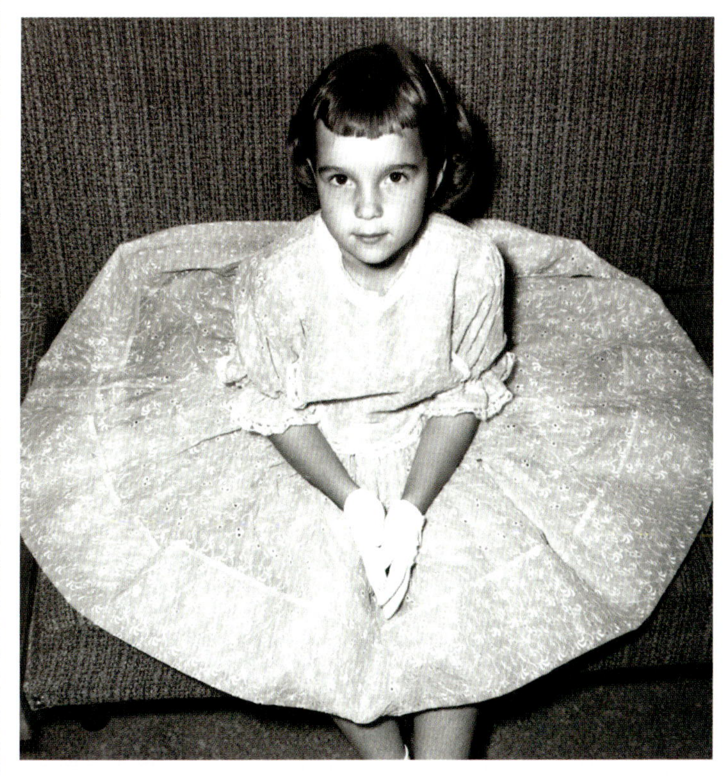

» Gail was a natural when it came to dressing up and posing for the camera. In addition to a variety of custom scenes which Mike created over the years, the grey blanket (seen above) was a frequent and familiar backdrop.

America's Cocktail Hour

In a body of work that deals with nostalgia, 320 35th Street is Gary's personal origin, but it's also ground zero of the American dream, a California creation myth. He was born "smack dab in the heart of America's euphoria. Here in the 'Greatest generation's glory days.' It is America's 'baby boom' with swing dancing, big bands, and post-World War II GIs. Southern California is ripe with beautiful people, movie stars, Walt Disney, the Beach Boys, white sports coats, pink carnations, high school proms, surfboards, beach parties, and slow cruisin' hot rods." [5]

In his description above, Gary's friend and fellow artist Ken Little moves seamlessly between place and time. The golden light of both form an alchemic buzz, America's cocktail hour, mixed with effervescent hope and the strong gin of war memory. This potent era fuels Gary's art. He uses time and memory to perform one of his favorite quotes by the painter Francis Bacon: "The job of the artist is to always deepen the mystery." [6]

Now in his 60s, Gary still looks the part of a California surfer—blonde hair, tanned skin, and strong physique. His affable nature is matched with an innate love for life; his sense of humor is matched with a kind sincerity.

"It wasn't exactly like a beach party movie, but it really was that carefree. We'd go down to the beach every day and surf in the morning when the water was glassy, then bring our mats and stuff down in the afternoon and stay there all day long," said Gary.

These are subjects made eponymous by the Beach Boys, yet even they weren't lucky enough to be born in South Bay. "They were 'flatlanders,'" said Gary. "They were from Hawthorne, the next town over, east of us. And only one of them (Dennis) surfed. Amazingly, they were never fully accepted as surfers, even though they introduced surf culture to the entire world."

RIGHT » Gary on the beach near his house. From there, he used the steep walkway (seen in photo on right) and walked three blocks to his house on the right (not shown).

I want to reproduce this picture 55 years later. None of the houses behind me in the younger image exist anymore. They're all McMansion vacation homes. I remember in the late 1970s a house sold for $1 million down there and everyone freaked out. When my parents bought their house, there were lots of empty lots on The Strand. My wife once asked my father, "Why didn't you buy a lot down there?" and he said, "Nobody wanted to live down there, it was all sandy and windy." Recently, a house was sold for $15 million and was razed to build a bigger, "better" house.

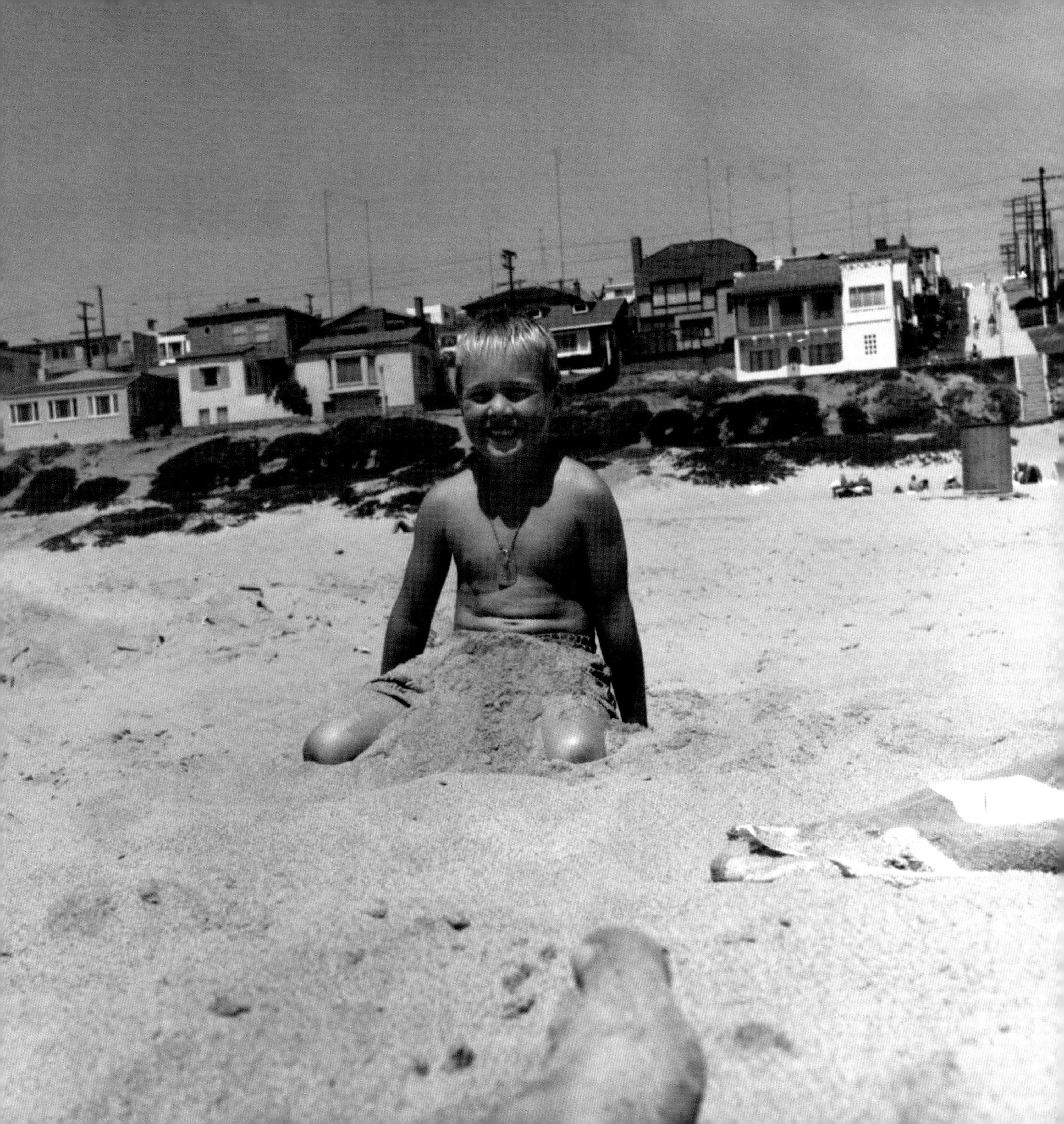

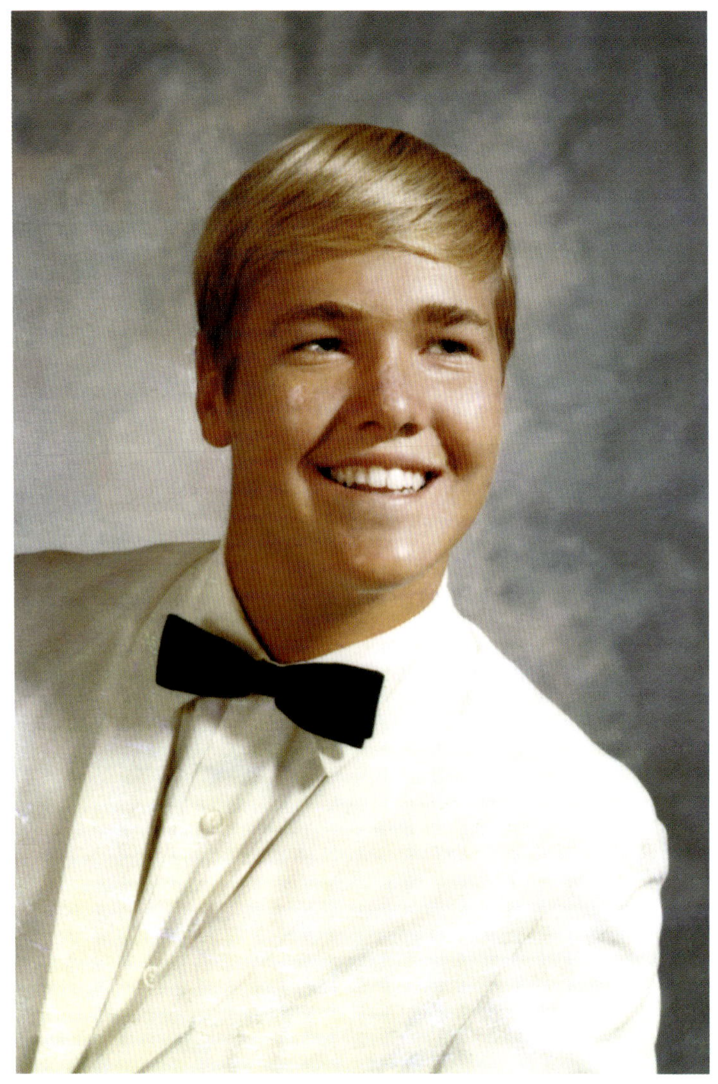

» Gary's prom pictures from an innocent time in the 1960s.

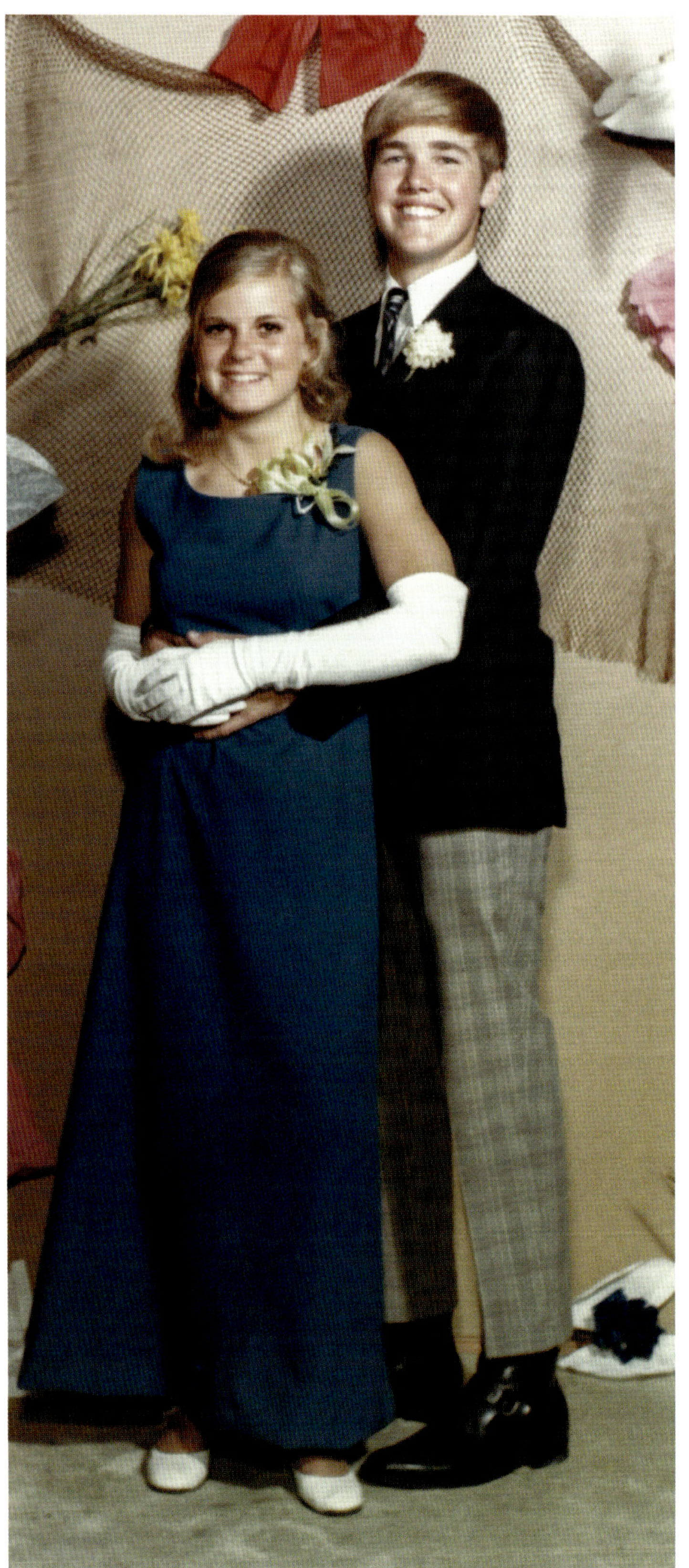

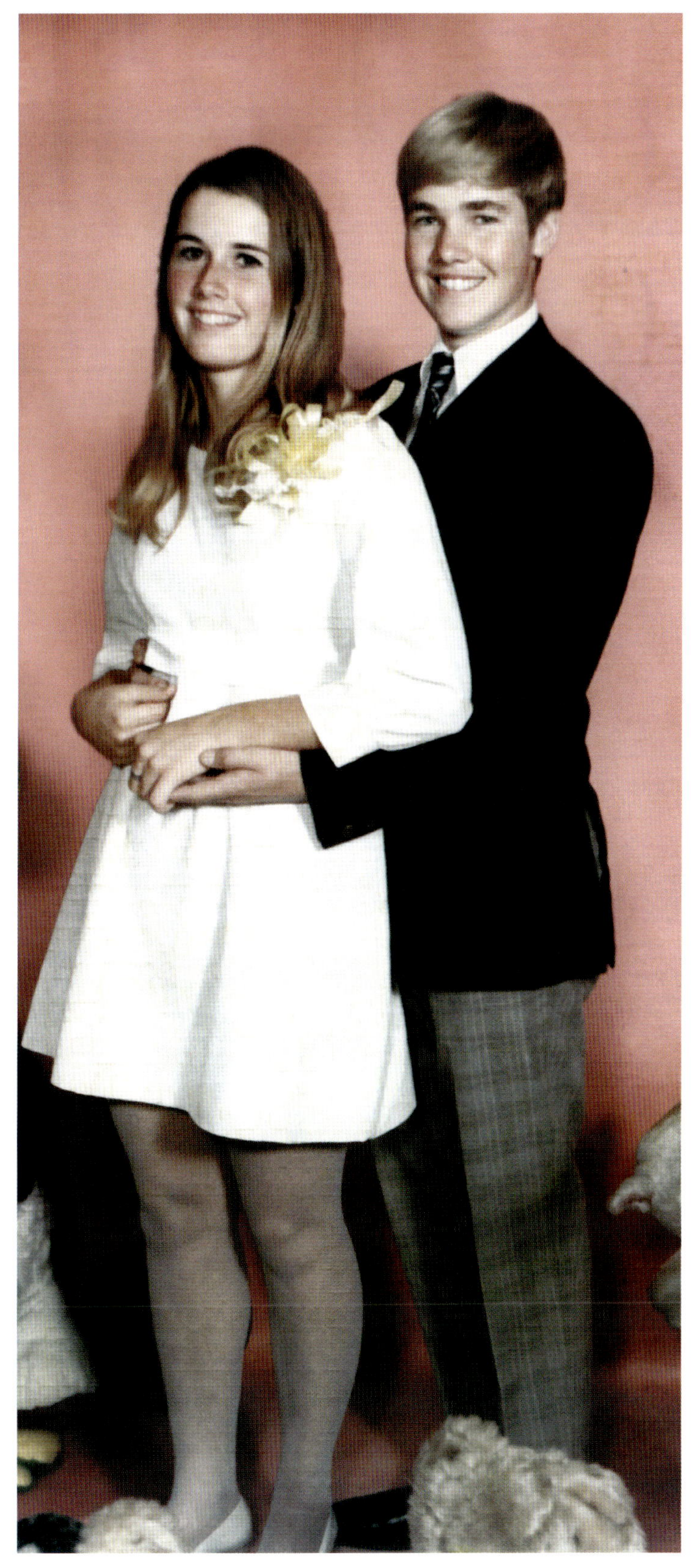

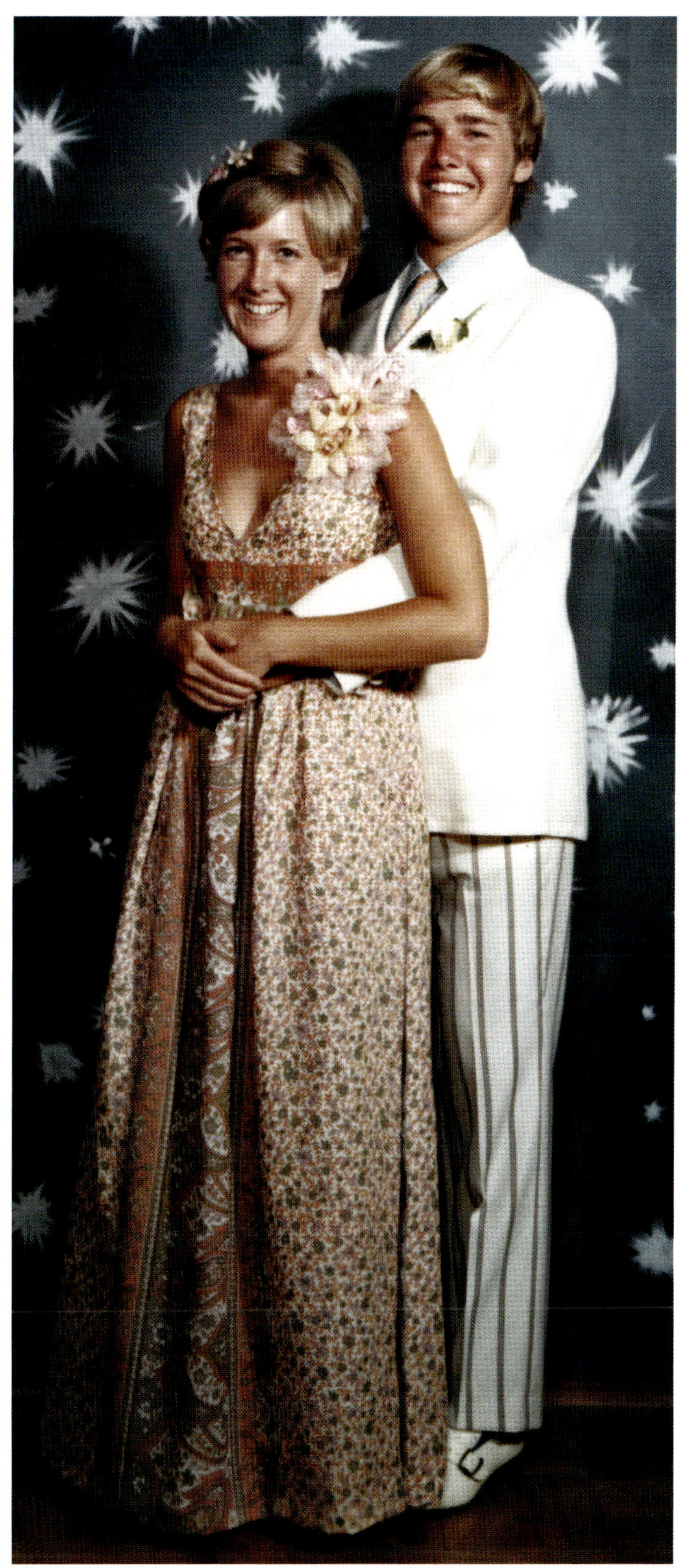

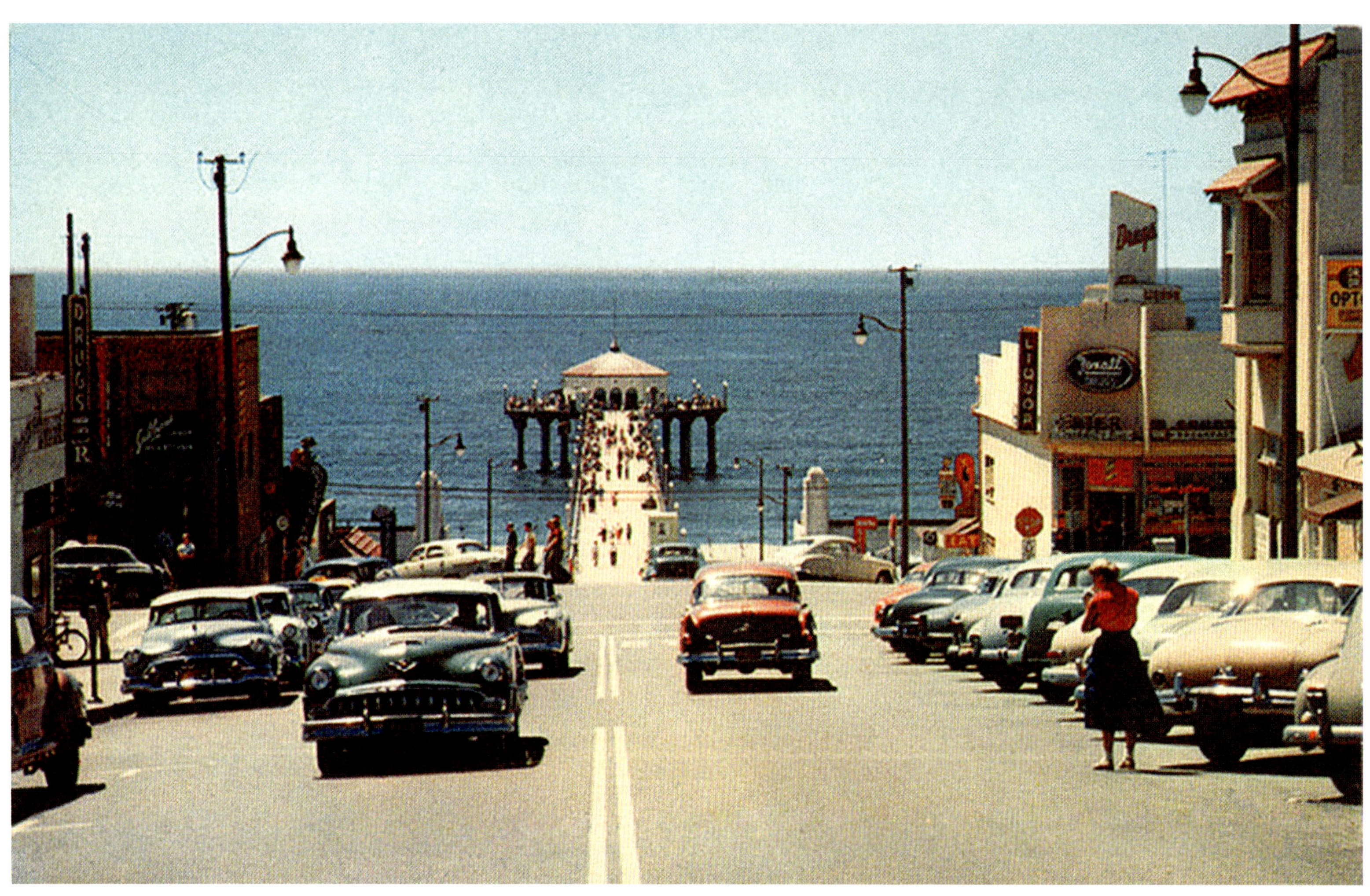
DRUGS
LIQUOR

Second City

While Gary was growing up, so was the California art scene. In 1957, Walter Hopps and Edward Kienholz started Ferus Gallery. Irving Blum would later replace Kienholz and eventually take over Hopps' role as well. He showed a stable of male artists that came to be known as the "Ferus Studs": John Altoon, Larry Bell, Billy Al Bengston, Bruce Conner, Joe Goode, Robert Irwin, Craig Kauffman, Kienholz, Kenneth Price, and Ed Ruscha. Hopps also showed New York Pop artists Andy Warhol and Jasper Johns.

"Almost all of these artists taught at UC Irvine. Many were my professors," said Gary. "Craig Kauffman, Ed Moses, James Turell. There wasn't a single West Coast arts student who wasn't influenced by John Baldessari [a Conceptual artist who worked with found photographs]. He taught at Cal-Arts and was responsible for most of the young art superstars of the 1980s."

Ferus Gallery was located in West Hollywood on La Cienega Boulevard. Cienega is the Spanish term for swamp or marshlands. Like the dunes of Manhattan Beach, the name hints of the geological history beneath it.

"Southern California, whose mythic status as the center of American pop culture—with Hollywood, hot rods, beaches, palm trees, blondes and suntans—epitomized the Pop environment."[7] Yet despite these connections, West Coast artists were continually marginalized. In the 1960s, Los Angeles was called the "second city" to New York, even as a distinct, West Coast version of Pop developed simultaneously with the East coast version.[8] Nancy Marmer articulated a specific kind of "L.A. look," which involved "high-polish craftsmanship and ... established conventions of decorative paint techniques."[9] Marmer used Ruscha's work as an example: "his combination of original imagery based on the signs and products of commerce with an impeccable lettering and design technique taken from advertising conventions brings him closer to 'pure' Pop than any other artists working in the style on the West Coast.'"[10]

The intellectual heaviness of the East Coast contrasted with the West Coast world. Conceptually, there is a horizontal aspect to West Coast art, as opposed to the layered history of the East Coast. As with the Pop and Finish Fetish styles, the content or subject was on the surface, like a beach horizon, washed away fresh every morning.

In the documentary, *The Cool School,* the surviving Ferus artists recall the beginnings of the West Coast art scene:

"We don't have to deal with our past because there is no past," said Baldessari.

"L.A. was a city of light and air and reflection," said Bengston.

"We weren't suffering like people do in New York City," said Baldessari. "Instead of being closed in and cramped together, California artists (like Ed Moses) painted outside." [11]

The California Light and Space Movement, started by Irwin, was inspired by the California light.

This freedom, mixed with the southern California climate, formed the rarified ecosphere that Gary was raised in. His grandmother, Maggie, was an artist who took him to galleries and museums—she took him to see Kienholz's *Back Seat Dodge '38* at the 1966 Los Angeles County Museum of Art exhibition.

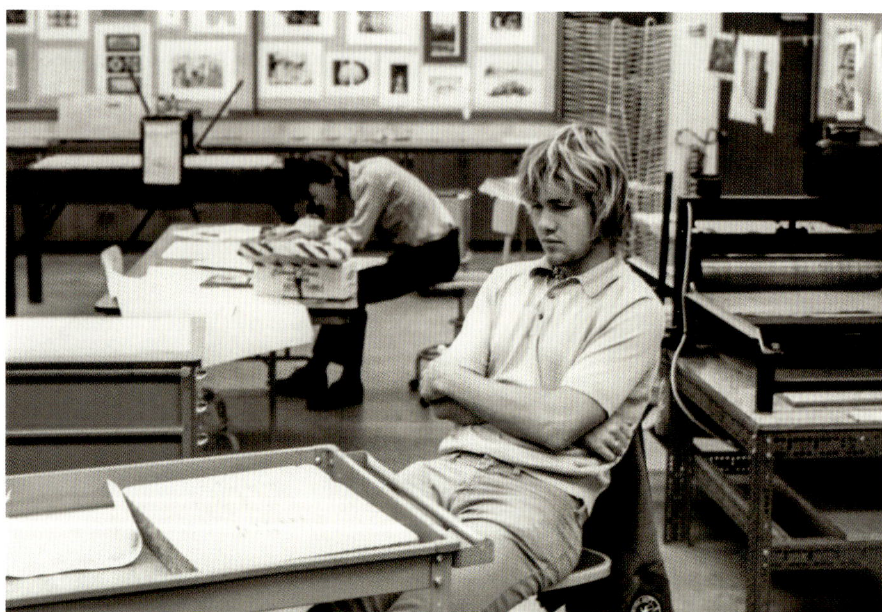

ABOVE » Staring at a lithostone in art class at UC Irvine, hoping for inspiration.

RIGHT » *How I misspent my youth.*

Gary was drawn to the California surf culture just as its mass popularity began.

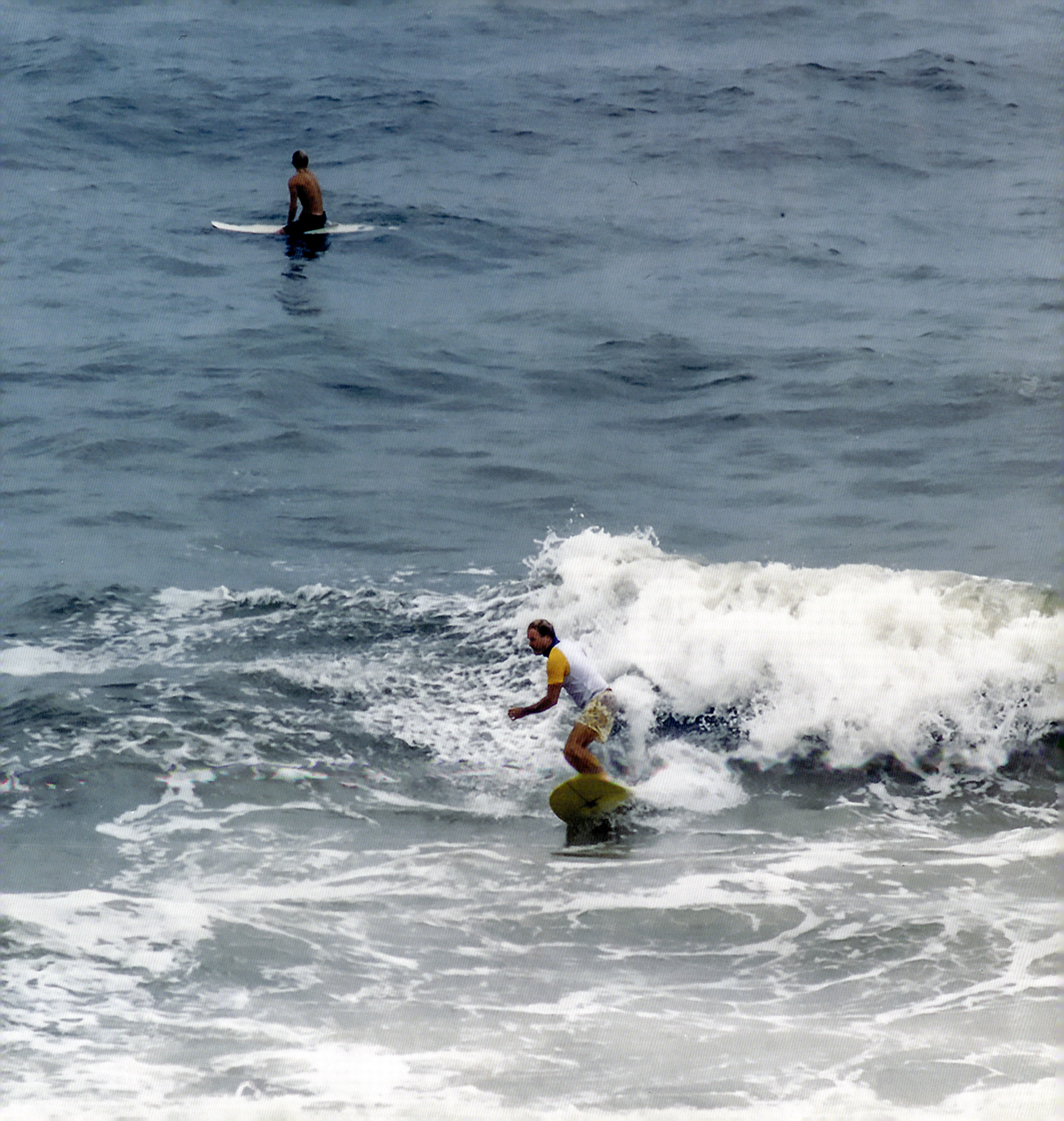

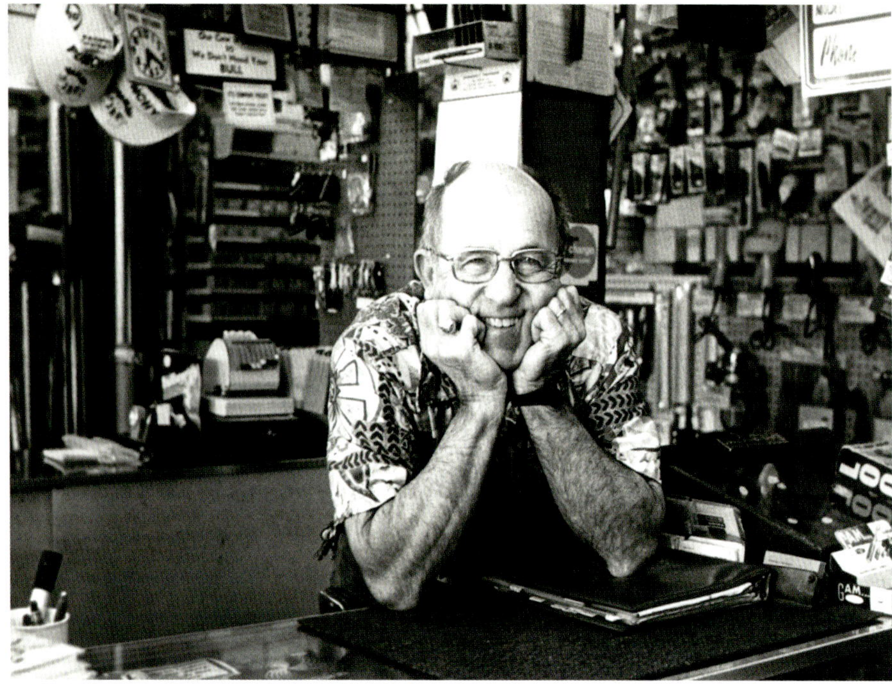

ABOVE » The affable Mike Sweeney at his hardware store.

It was a typical small town hardware store with narrow aisles and stuff jammed from floor to ceiling. It had a workbench in back where customers came to work on projects. My father could solve any home repair problem. Since he was the mayor, it was also a hub for political scuttlebutt and gossip.

RIGHT » North end of Manhattan Beach. Sweeney's Hardware is in the building just before Cisco's, a music venue owned by Dick Smothers and Clint Eastwood.

On Friday and Saturday nights, the place was hopping. It was the cabaret area. Ike and Tina Turner played there several times—Glenn Campbell, everyone that was popular—Cheech and Chong, the First Edition. It was a hotbed of early '70s music.

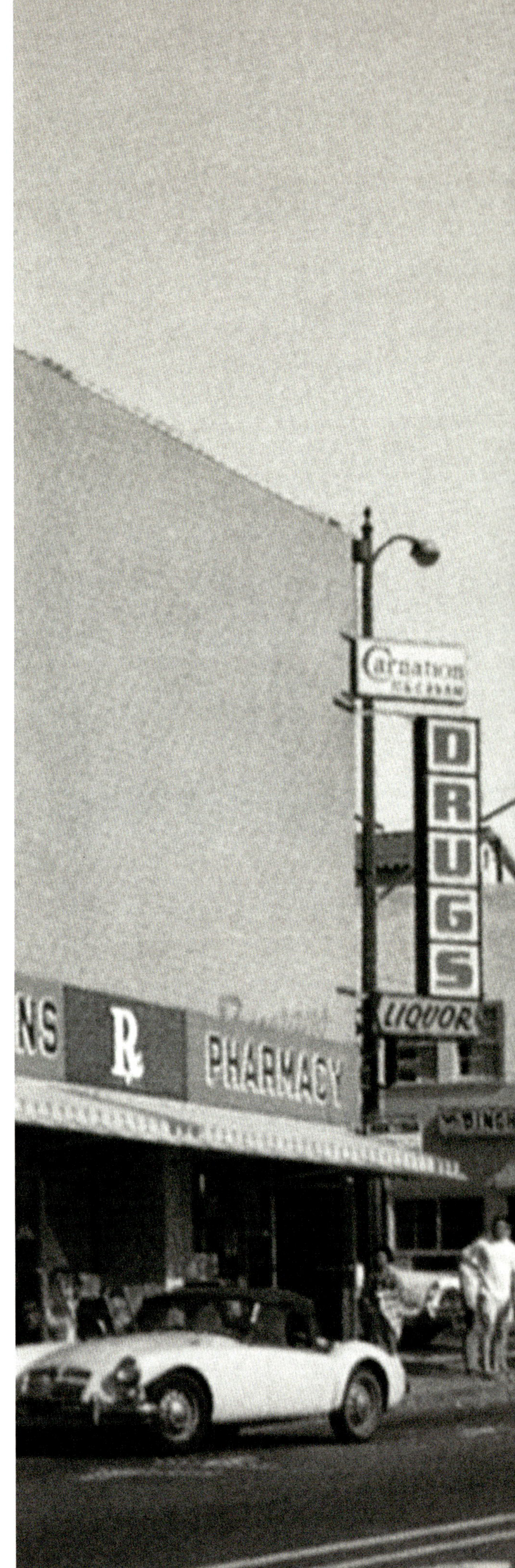

Manhattan Beach, California

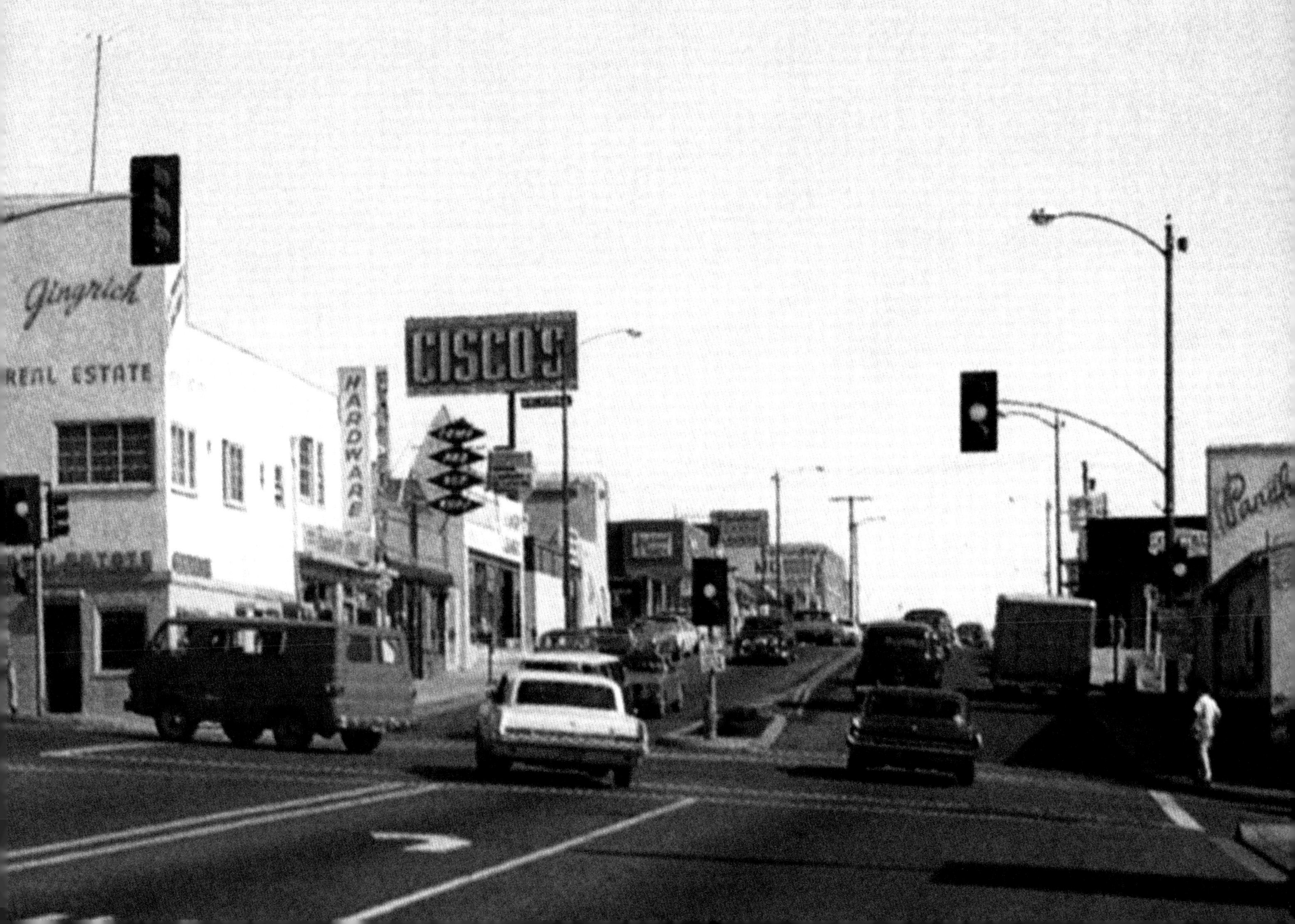

Road Trips

In 1964, Gary's father bought a Ford Econoline van and the family took a 9,000-mile road trip across the country. They drove along Route 66, past the gas stations memorialized by Ruscha in his 1962 photo book, *26 Gas Stations,* experiencing all of the "banal yet mythic themes—the car, the road, the American vernacular landscape," all subjects that would be incorporated into West Coast Pop aesthetic. [12]

"It was a keystone moment in my life," said Gary. "We went all the way up to Maine, we went to New York City, to MoMA, where I saw Robert Rauschenberg's goat with a tire going through it [*Monogram* (1955-59)]. It stopped me in my tracks. This vacation made such an impression on me."

Architectural critic Reyner Banham described the West coast's urban landscape as "distinguished by three characteristics: mobility, speed and newness." [13] Banham defined "'gestalt' as the inhabitant's physical, psychological and perceptual experience of the city." These same elements were the subjects of West Coast art—Ruscha's paintings, Bell's optical sculptures, Kauffman's iridescent Plexiglas sculptures.

The road trip would continue to be an important part of Gary's life. When he was sixteen, he rode his bicycle from Manhattan Beach to San Francisco, and then when he graduated from Mira Costa High School in 1970, he took another epic road trip, this time with his friend Mike Downs. Together, they rode across the country, from West to East Coast, on their bicycles.

"The most amazing thing is that our parents were completely into it. We just had basic ten-speeds. We were so loaded up that sometimes, going downhill, the front wheel of my bike would lift up off the ground," said Gary. "Can you imagine a parent letting their child do that today?"

His art is steeped in the California vernacular and a South Bay "gestalt" of sun and surf mixed with a West Coast Pop aesthetic. Like Baldessari, he uses found photographs, the ones from his father's archive. The subject matter is far from angst; it reflects the world he grew up in.

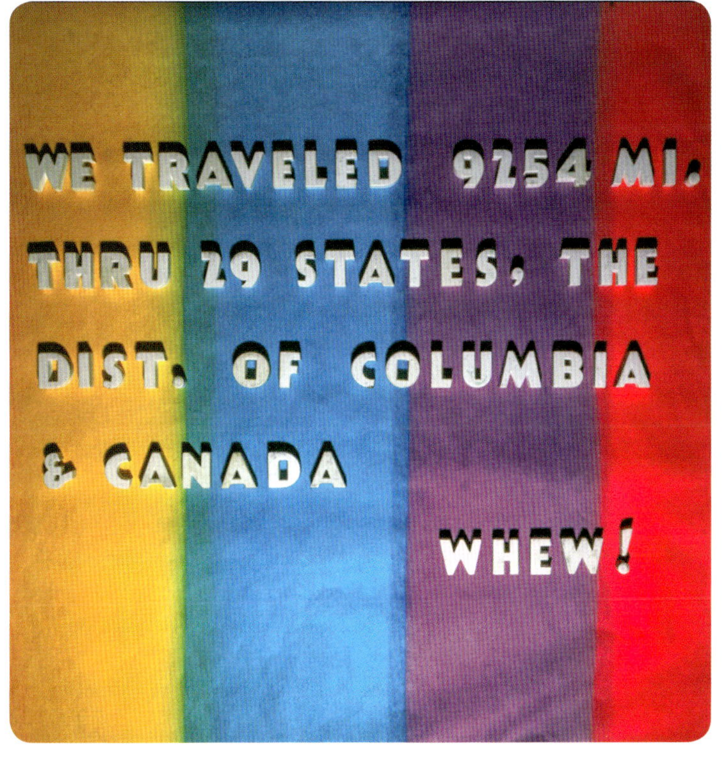

» Title slide for the 1964 marathon family road trip

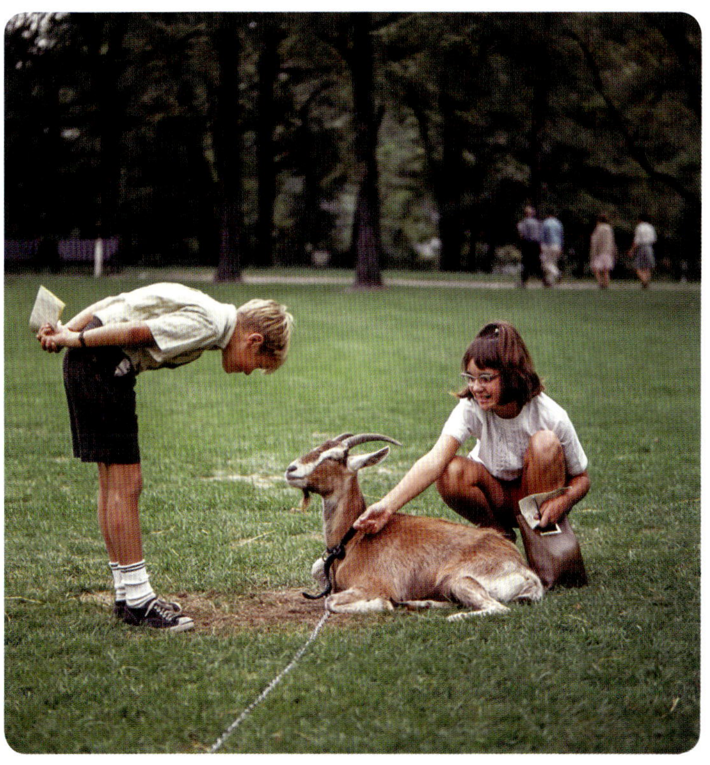

» The Henry Ford Museum, Dearborn, MI

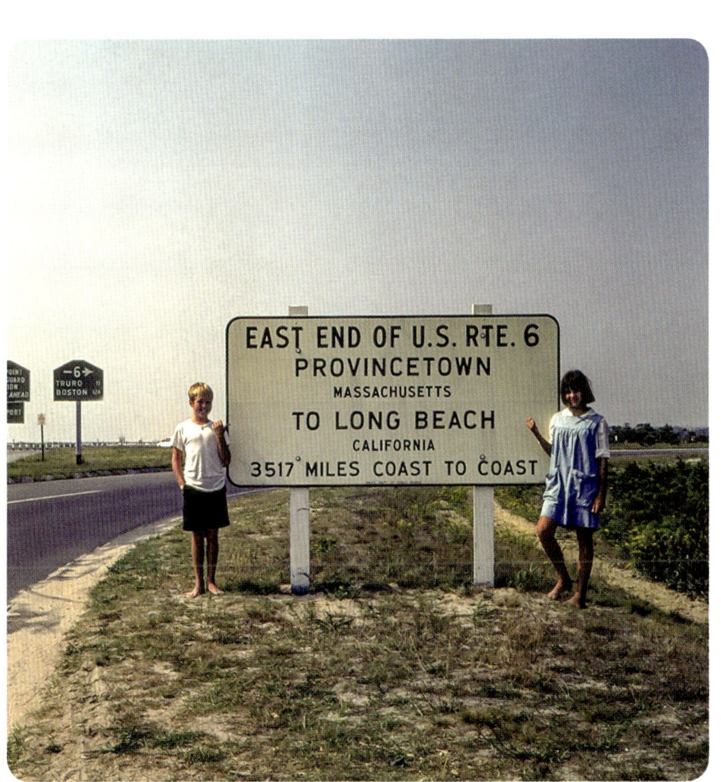

» The end of Cape Cod, MA

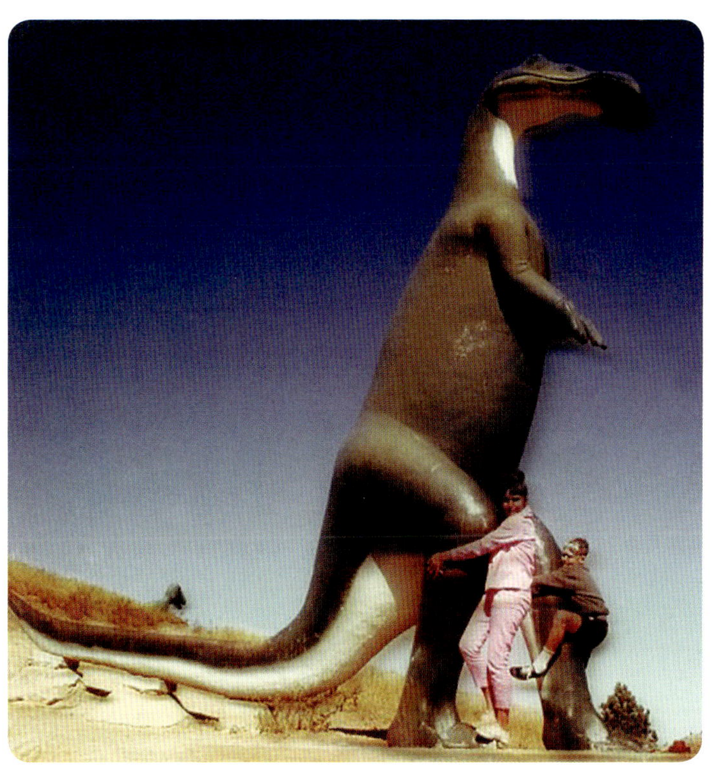

» Giant dinosaurs in the California desert

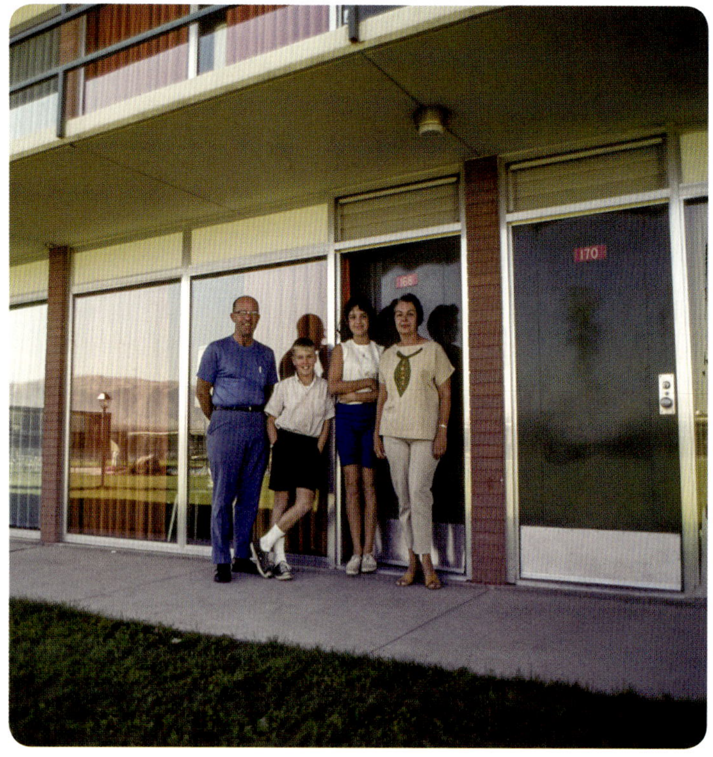

» Salt Lake City, UT

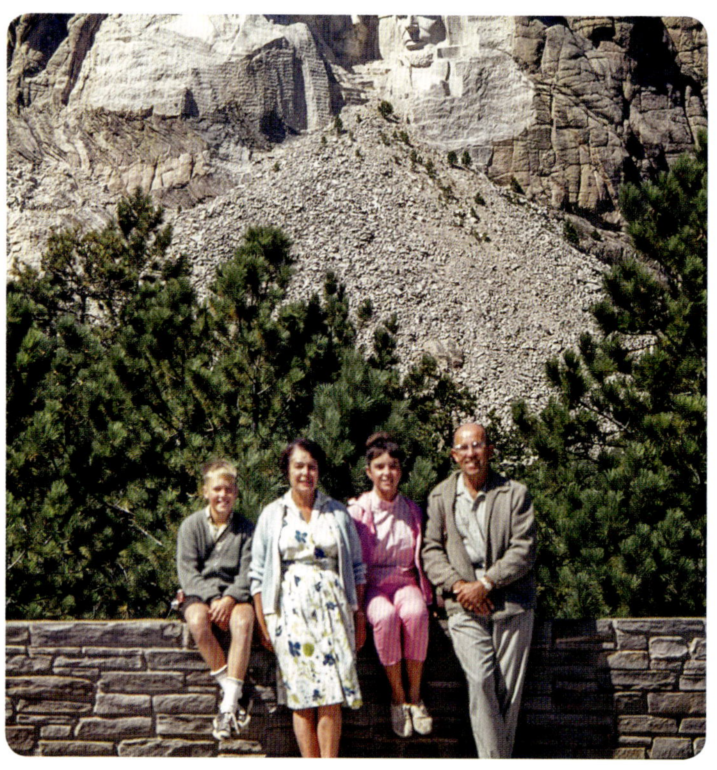

» Mt. Rushmore

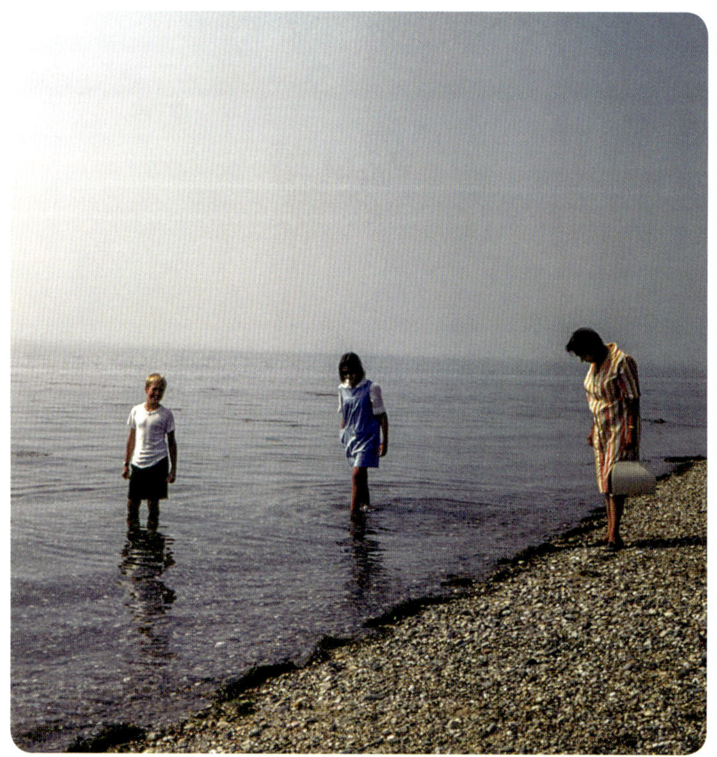

» Dipping our toes in the Atlantic Ocean at Cape Cod

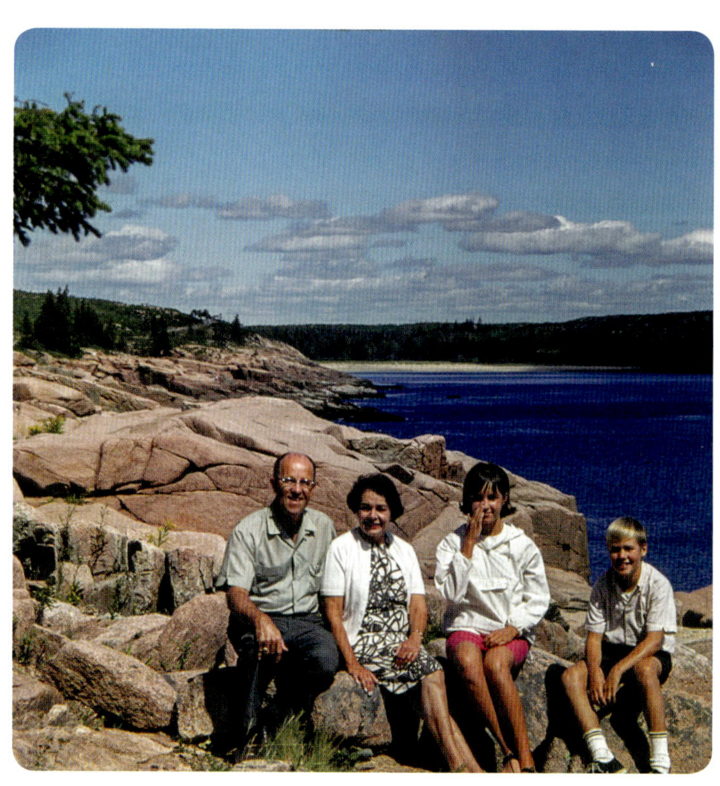

» The furthest point in our trip, Bar Harbor, ME

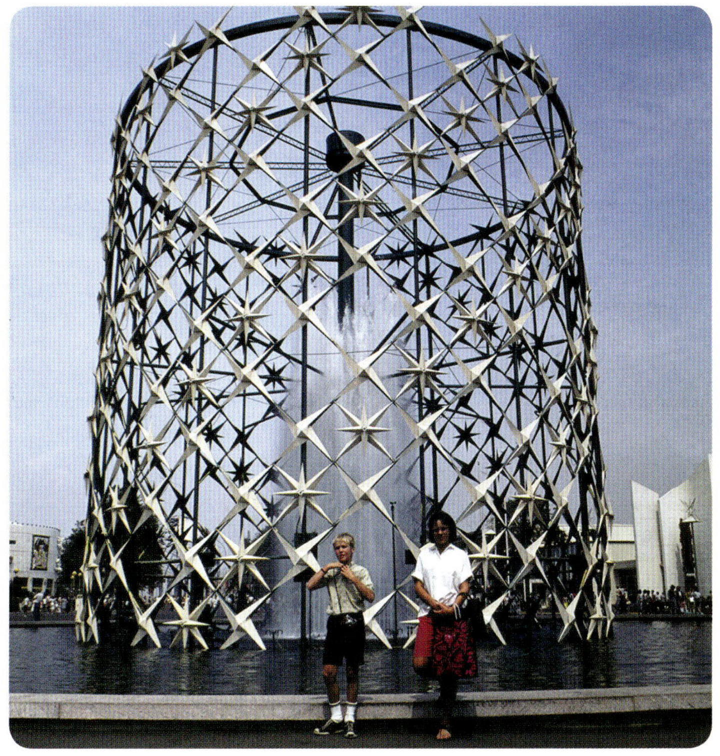

» 1964 New York World's Fair

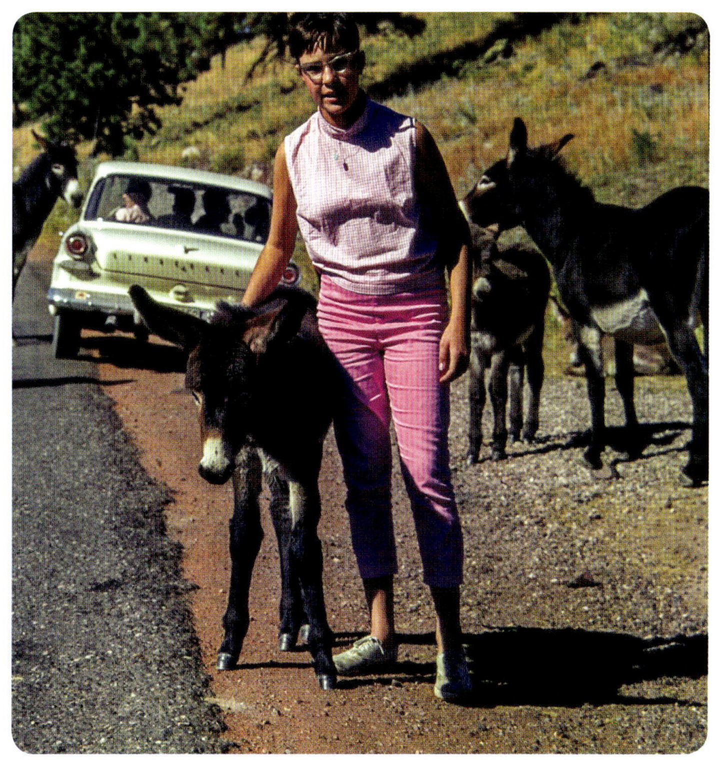

» Badlands of South Dakota

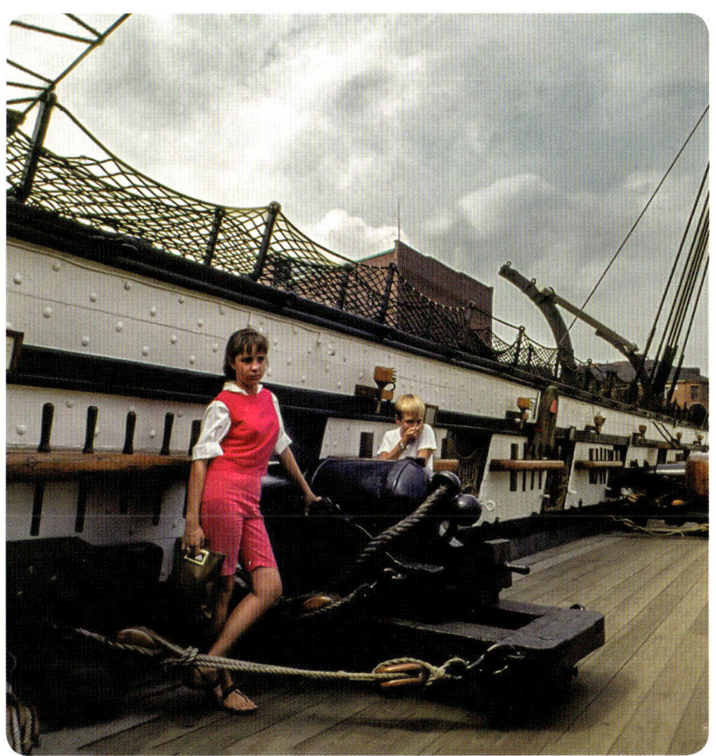

» USS Constitution ("Old Ironsides") in Boston Harbor

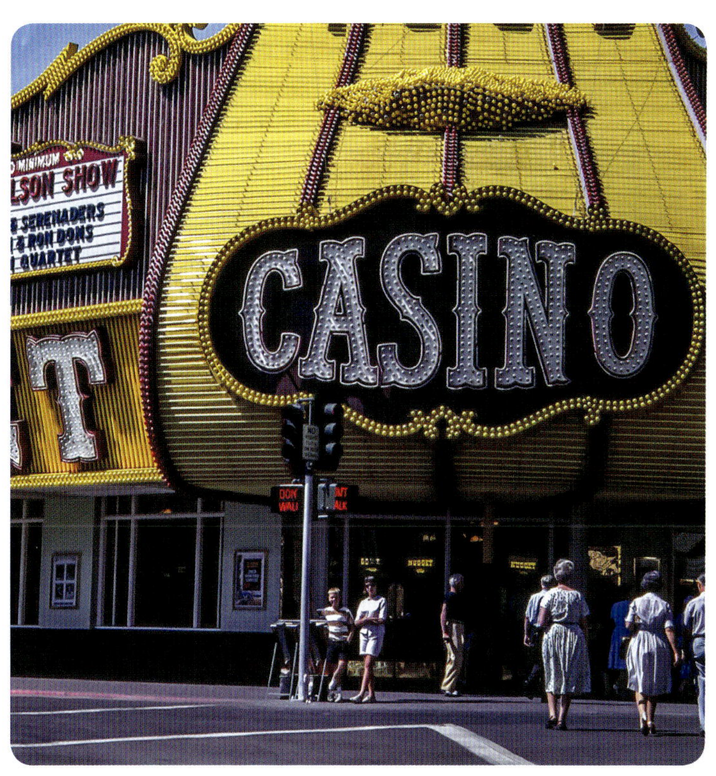

» Final stop, Las Vegas

RIGHT » In 1970, Gary and his friend Mike Downs spent 33 days traveling 3,200 miles from Manhattan Beach to Washington, D.C. on their bicycles.

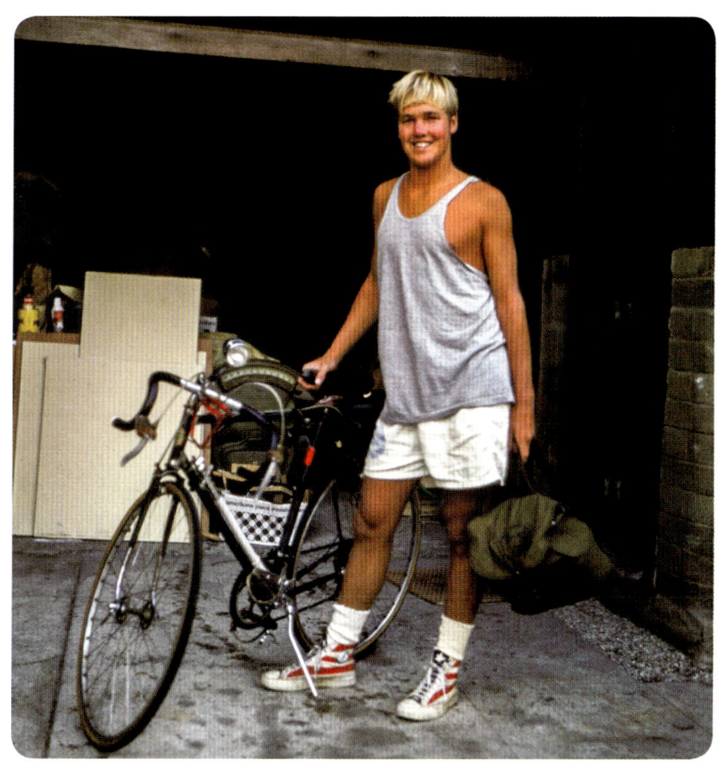
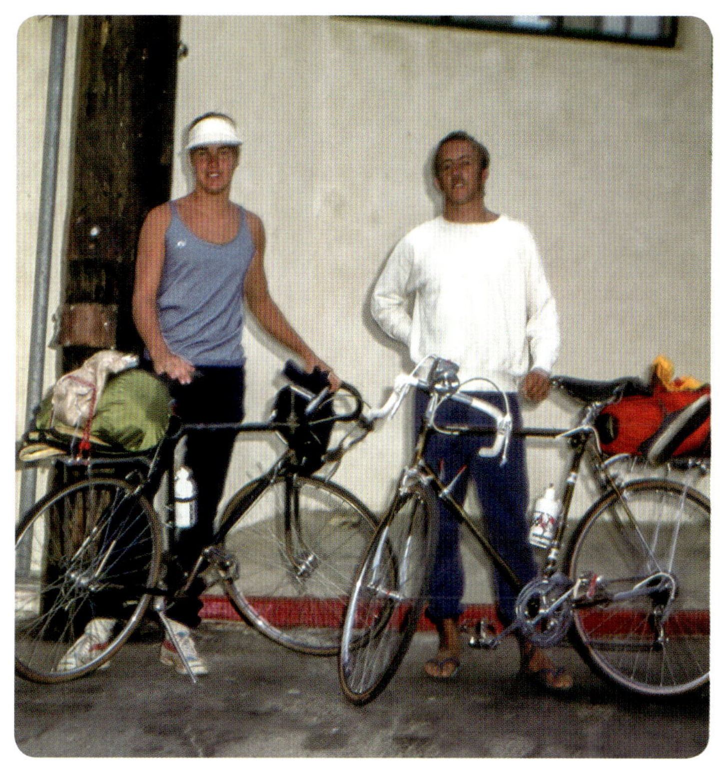
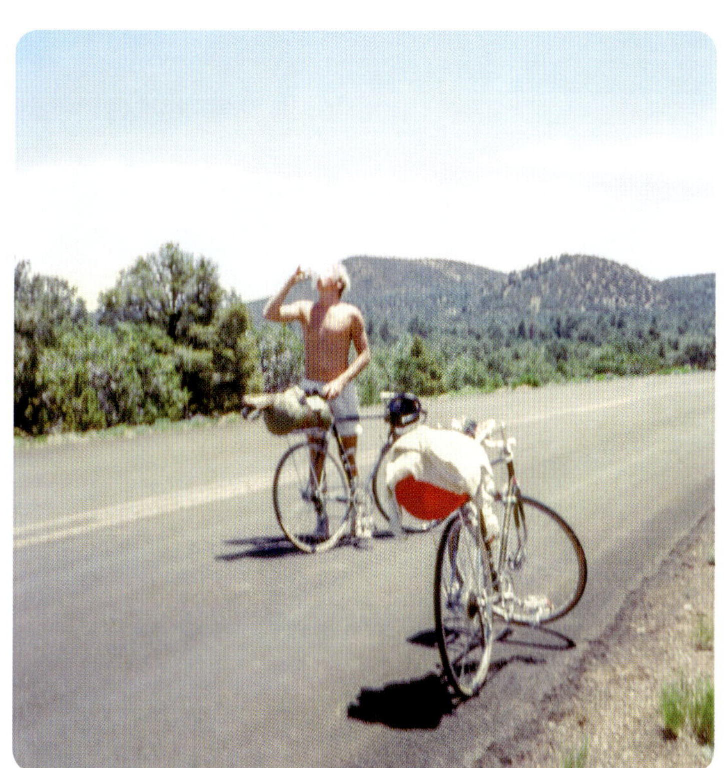
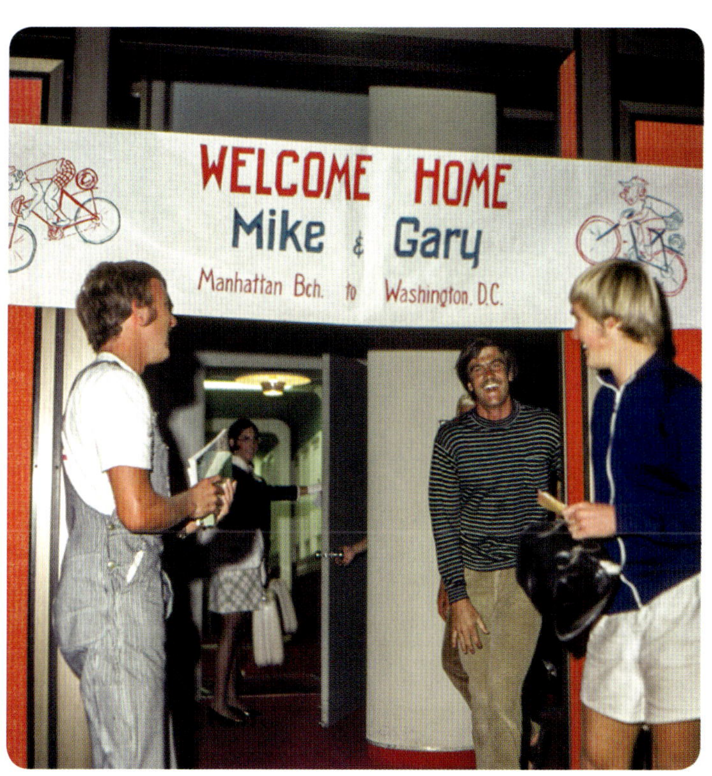
WELCOME HOME
Mike & Gary
Manhattan Bch. to Washington, D.C.

Cocker Spaniels and Casseroles

Our visual memory, the mind's eye, exists near the visual cortex in our brain. In the age of digital media, our exposure to images has profoundly increased. Yet, our mind's capacity somehow expands wide enough to catalog this abundance of images.

"Images trigger our memory of the history of images," wrote photographer and art historian Teju Cole.[14] One image is a referent of another image, which may lead to another, ad infinitum. The way our minds link visual images is like the Internet, an endless hall of mirrors, but the path we choose to go down depends on our own specific set of associations.

The more particular and specific the detail, the more it may prompt a personal connection. In the family's archives, it's a recipe from Gary's mother's folder, a homemade birthday cake decorated by his mother, a Halloween costume, or a pet. All hold familiar truths. Beyond their autobiographical function, the images are referents.

There's a large number of cocker spaniels in the family photo archive. Mostly, it's Cappy, who also has his own portrait. But also, there are pictures of Gary as a little boy posing with a litter of cocker spaniels.

"We always had to have a cocker spaniel. It was the '50s—everybody had to have one," said Gary.

The 1950s was known as an era of conformity, which author Thomas Pynchon satirizes in his novels. Pynchon lived in Manhattan Beach during the late 1960s and was close friends with Gary's sister, Gail. He mined southern California culture for material that appears in his novels *The Crying of Lot 49, Vineland,* and *Inherent Vice.*

RIGHT » Gary dressed as Davey Crockett with his cocker spaniel, Cappy.

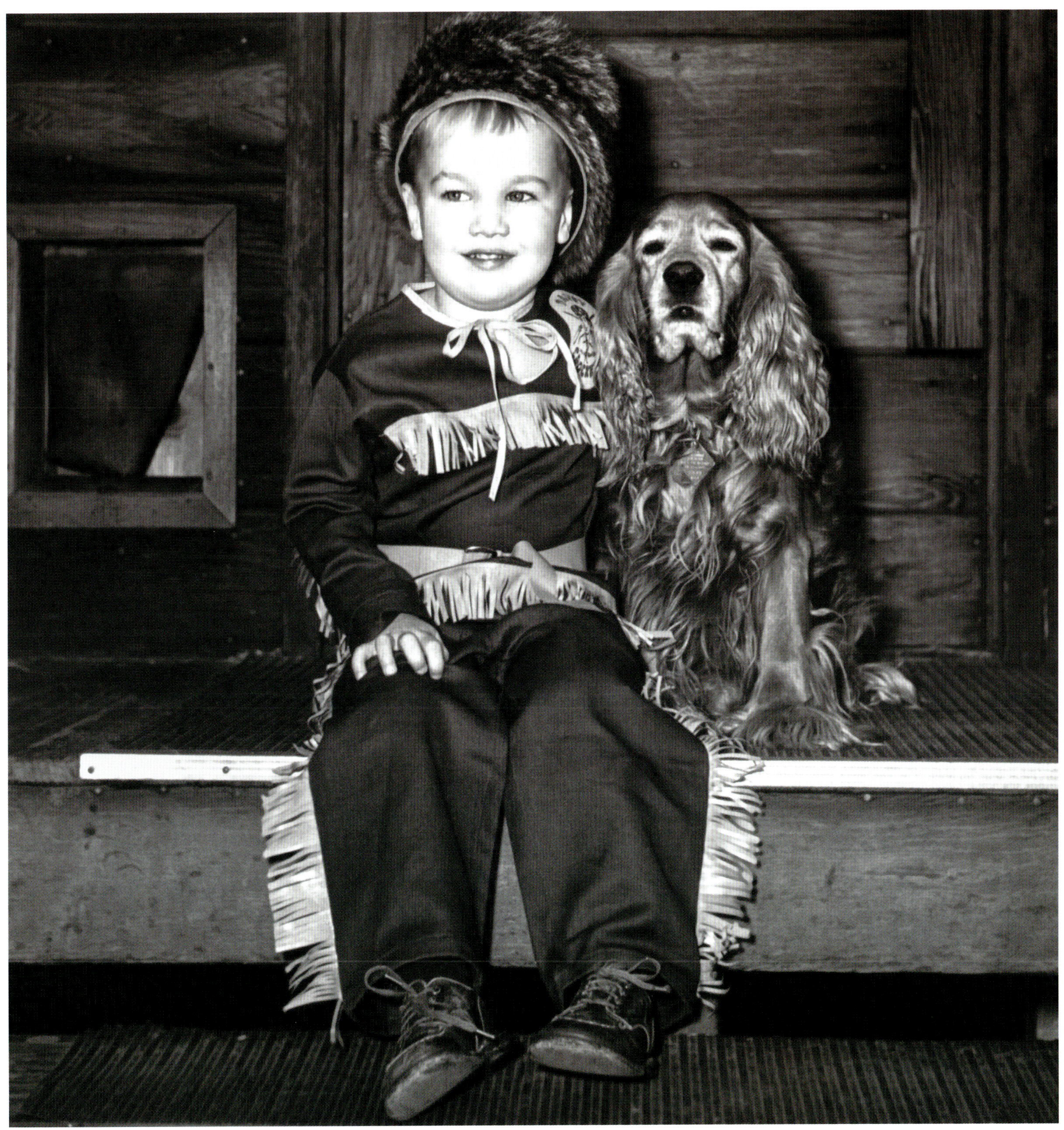

"The surfers in *Vineland* are based on my surfer friends," said Gary. "And he also has my mother's Spinach Casserole recipe in there."

Here it is:

> The secret to Spinach Casserole was the UBI, or Universal Binding Ingredient, cream of mushroom soup, whose presence in rows of giant cans there in the ninjette storeroom came as no surprise. Deep in the refrigerators were also to be scavenged many kinds of pieces of cheese, not to mention cases full of the more traditional Velveeta and Cheez Whiz, nor was spinach a problem, with countless blocks of it occupying their own wing of the freezer. So next day the classic recipe was the vegetarian entrée du jour at supper.[15]

The original recipe for this casserole was developed by Campbell's Soup Company, to promote use of their product, Cream of Mushroom Soup. Pynchon's "UBI" is a clever brand for that unforgettable gloppy, creamy, gravy-like substance that makes every other ingredient that it's mixed with taste palatable. Velveeta and Cheez Whiz are also included, both signature foods of Pop culture. Warhol's *Campbell's Soup Cans* and Ruscha's painting of Spam, *Actual Size,* were both created in 1962.

Pynchon's writing is the literary counterpart to Warhol and Ruscha's playful, sly appropriations. Gary also uses humor and appropriation to make the viewer see anew. The old pictures transform his home into a time capsule that shocks us into realizing how much has changed. In the catalog for his 40-year retrospective in 2013, Catherine Walworth described Gary as "a time traveler ... a *bricoleur,* a ragpicker, a tinkerer who takes old things and finds new uses for them. Therein lies his artistry, wrapped in a pun, wrapped in a Boy Scout badge. He uses the pleasant mask of insidious eras to remind us of our own cultural foibles."[16]

RIGHT » Traditionally Anita made birthday cakes for the family. An exception was the ice cream cake (top right) purchased from the local 31 Flavors which is still operating today.

FOLLOWING » *We were accustomed to wearing costumes and posing for the camera.*

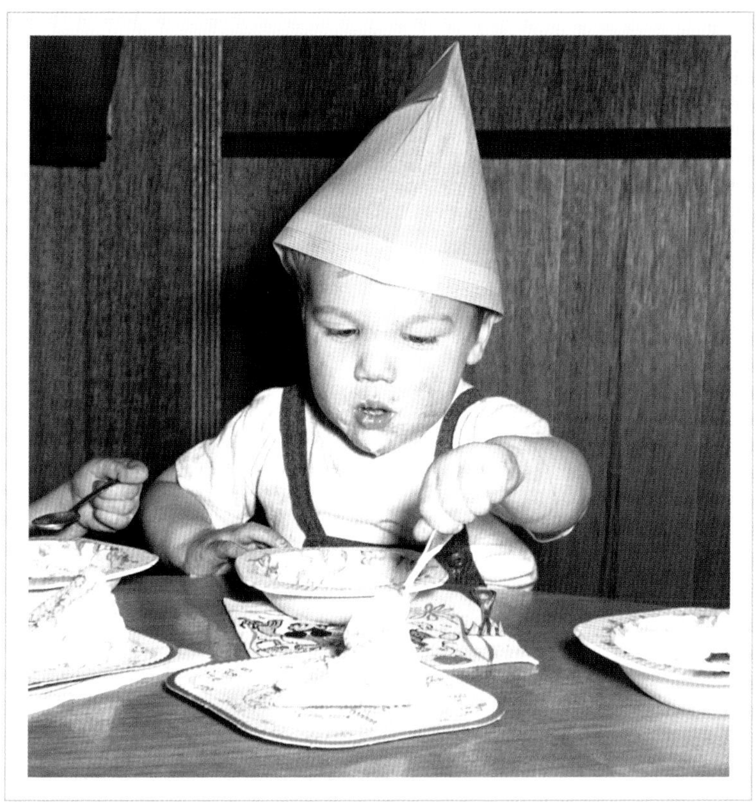

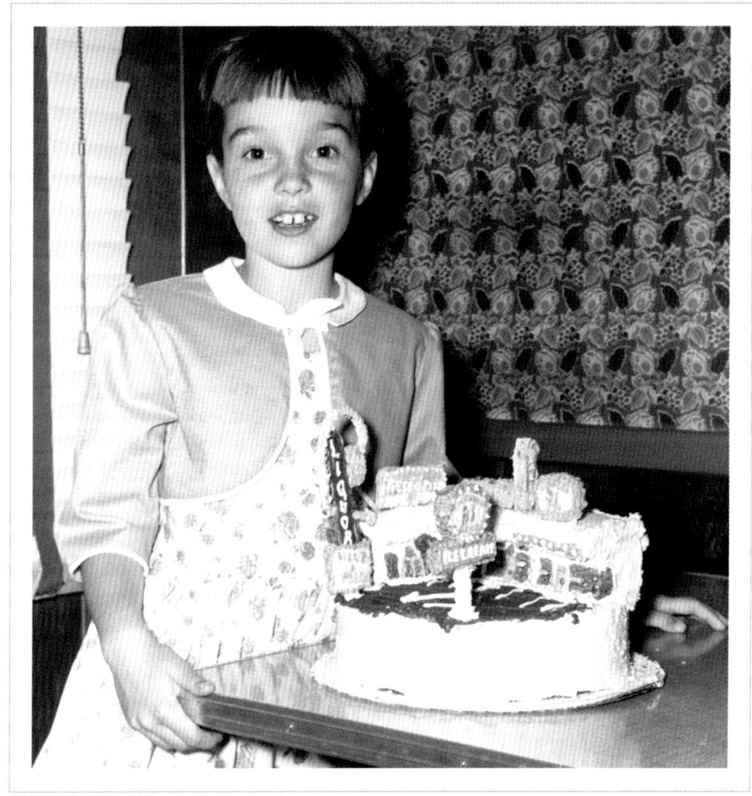

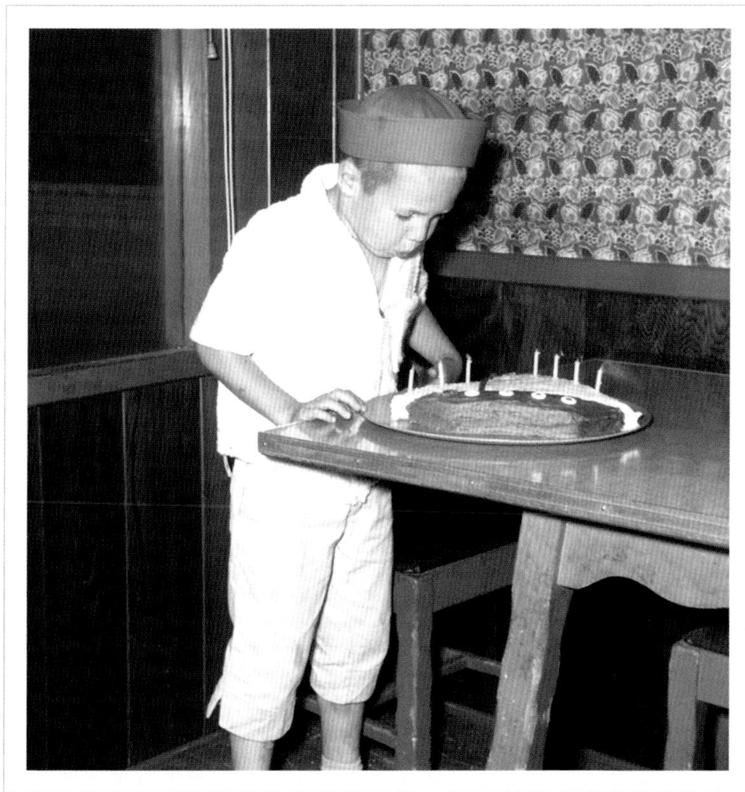

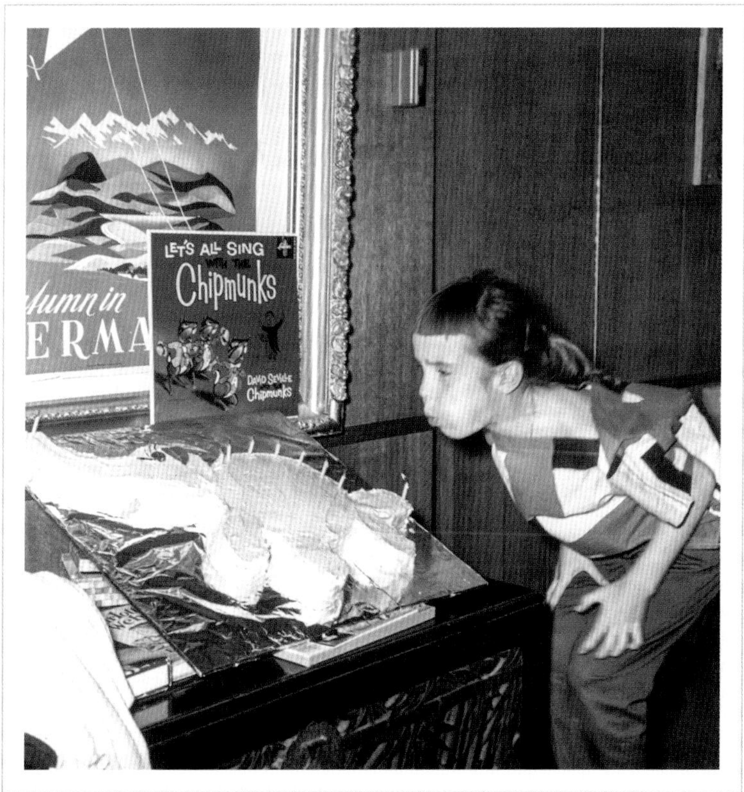
LET'S ALL SING
Chipmunks
DAVID SEVILLE
Chipmunks

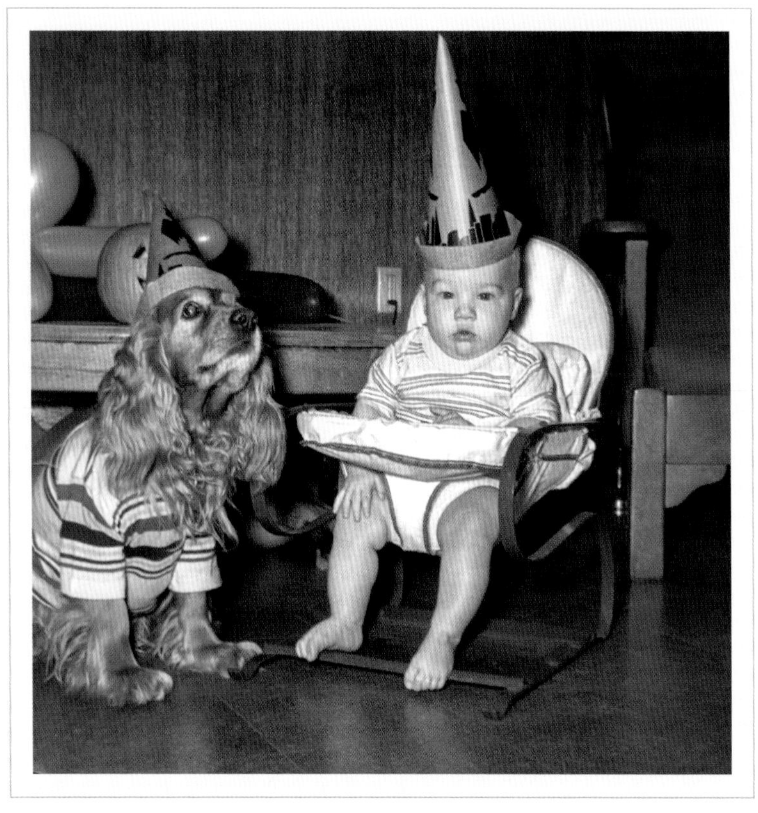
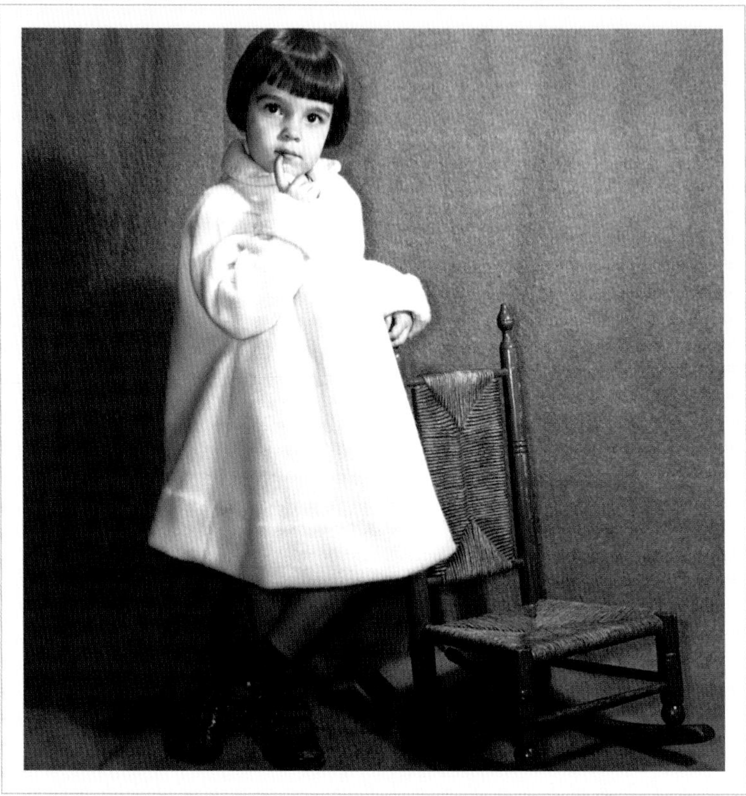
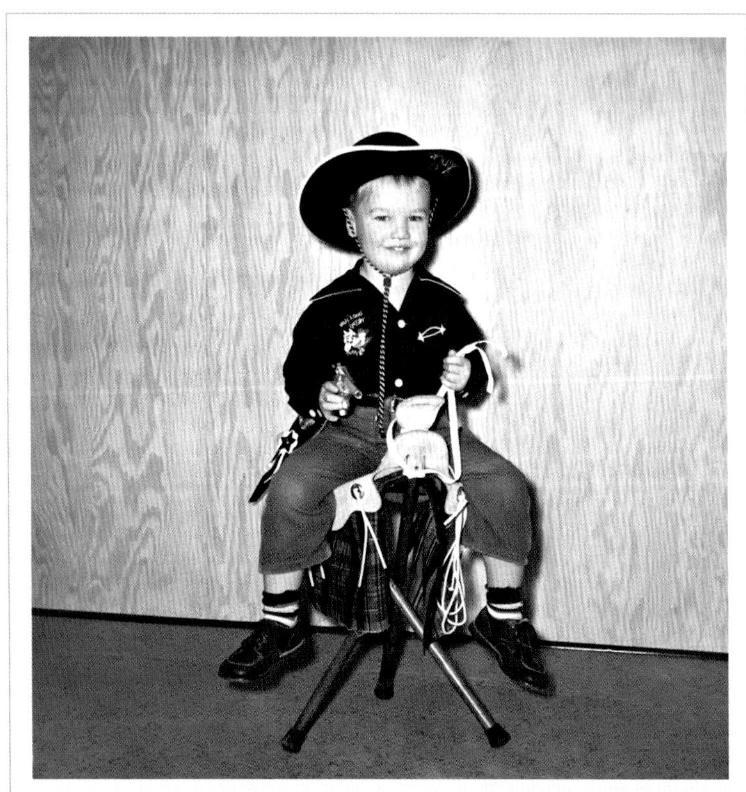
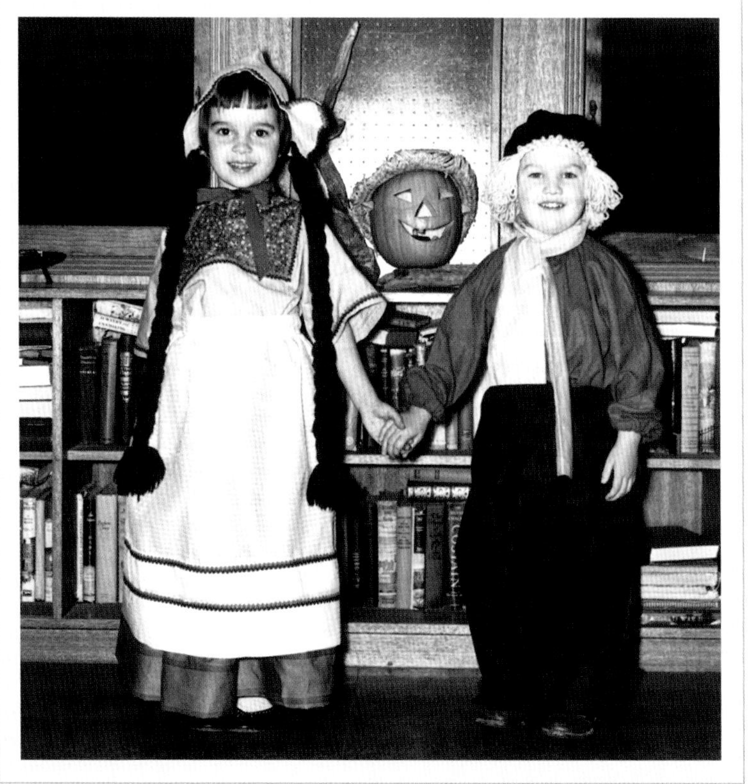

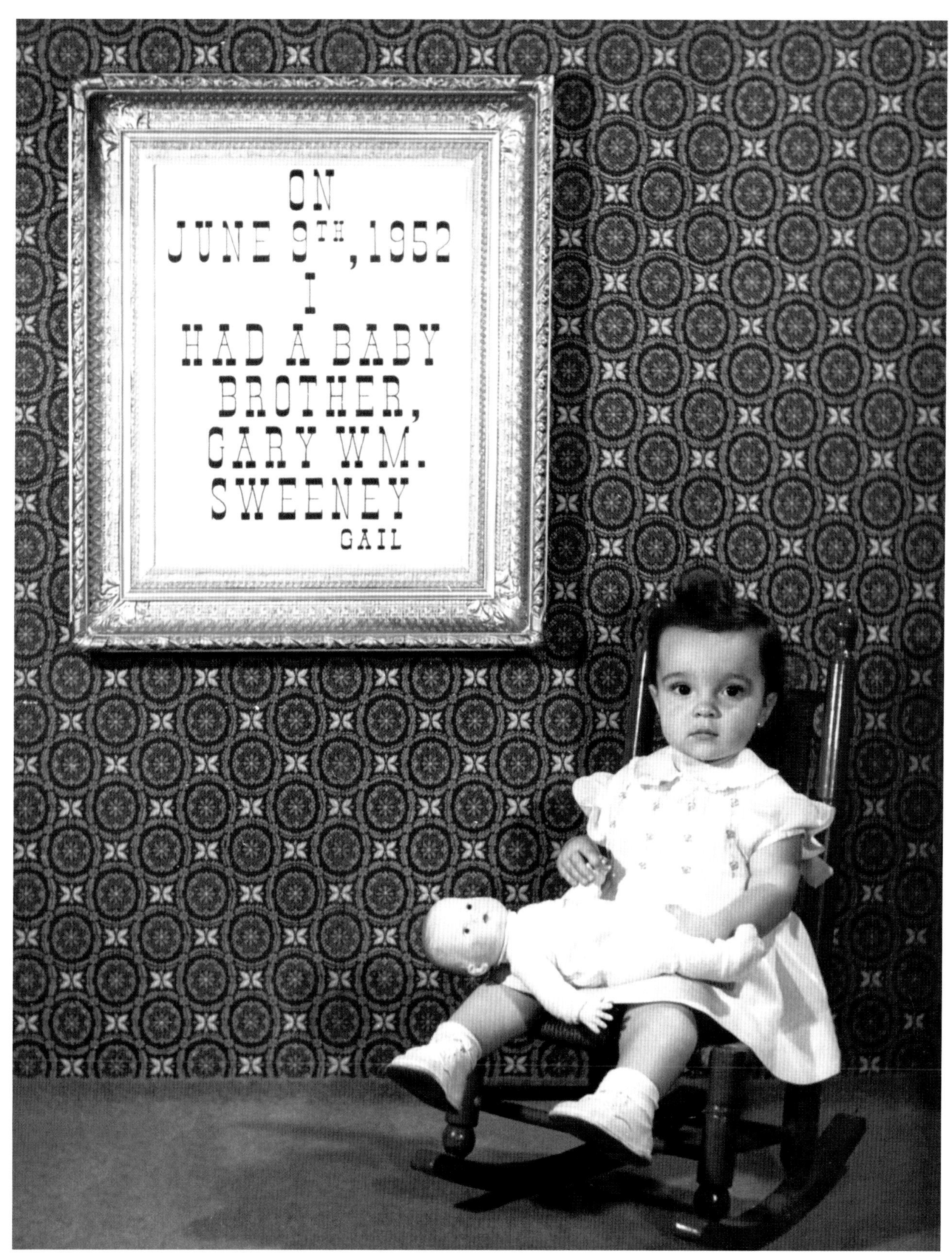
ON
JUNE 9TH, 1952
I
HAD A BABY
BROTHER,
GARY WM.
SWEENEY
GAIL

Memory Triggers

Gary selected photos that centered around or featured his home: his first day of school, Christmas morning opening his Erector Set, his father under the magnolia tree that he received as a gift for his service with the PTA. He culled them from the vast collection that he inherited from his father. These family images have been a subject in his art ever since he created *America—Why I Love Her* (1994), a public art installation at the Denver airport that featured the photos from his epic family road trip taken in the Econoline van. For the installation, he created a giant map of the U.S. and put up the family photos that were taken at all of the strange roadside attractions and eccentric museums they visited.

"'This series was the first exhibit that reflected my personality and my personal life, and I'm still doing it, so that exhibit changed my career,'" said Gary.[17]

"'I've been using nostalgia in my art forever. People can relate to that family vacation stuff—driving around in a station wagon in the '50s and '60s. I don't want to highlight my family as much as trigger memories. My family wasn't unique. We were ridiculously typical—two kids, a dog. I played Little League, was in Boy Scouts, joined all the things kids did back then.'"[18]

Gary's personal photos tell his story but also prompt viewers' memories of their own. When we step outside our own shoes and view life through someone else's lens, what we see about our own lives becomes more perceptible. Joseph Campbell calls this the "transcendent through the transparent." This same ingredient lures people to scroll infinitely downwards on Facebook. The photos posted may have nothing to do with us, but there is always some detail to identify with, however random. Sharing images in the virtual world can lead to an anonymous form of spying, but sharing images in the real world, as Gary did, led to real connections, conversations, and re-connections.

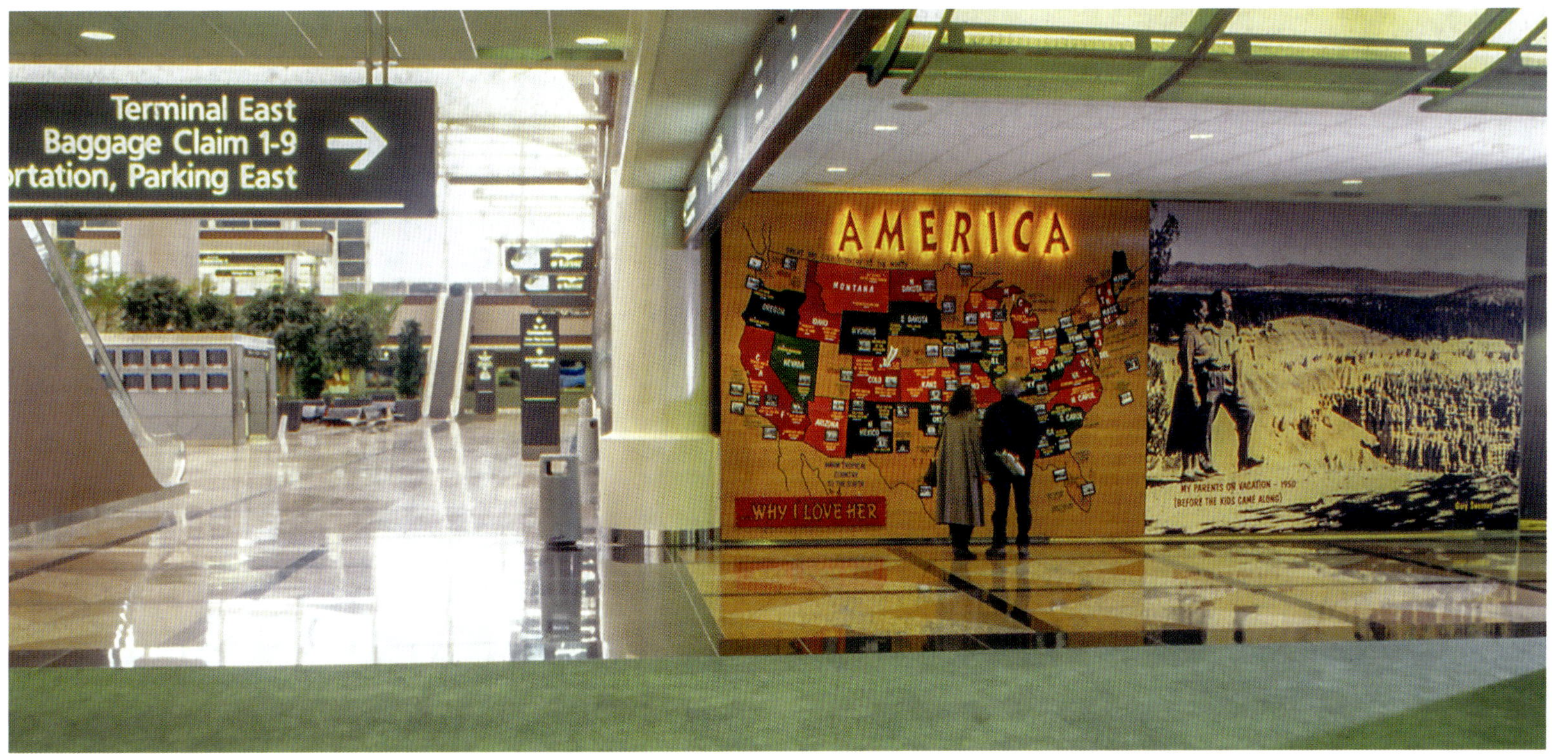

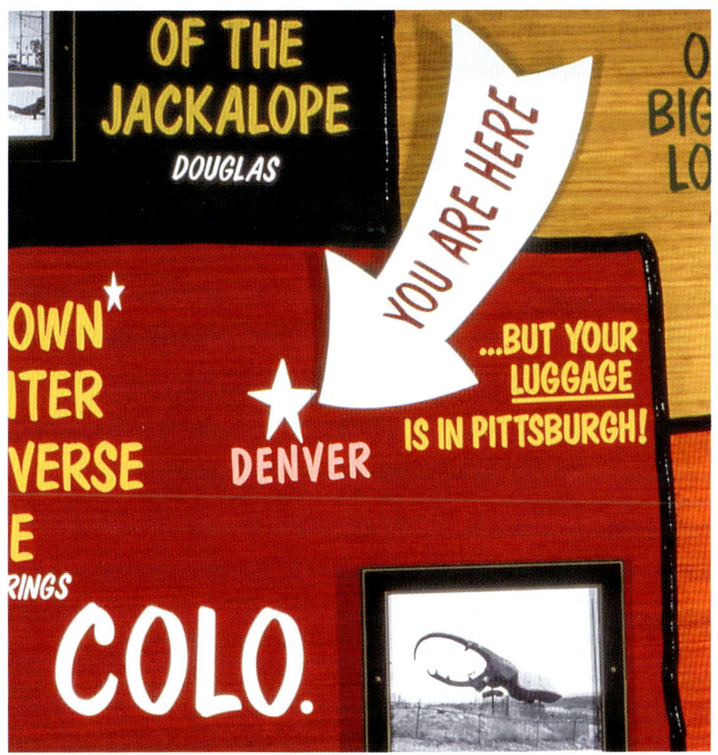

Gary's installation, *America, Why I Love Her* (1992), at the Denver International Airport

ABOVE & LEFT » Installation and detail views of northern wall of corridor between main terminal and baggage claim

FOLLOWING » Southern wall of corridor

Because of the abundant supply of material and inspiration, family vacations became an endless theme in my artwork as an adult.

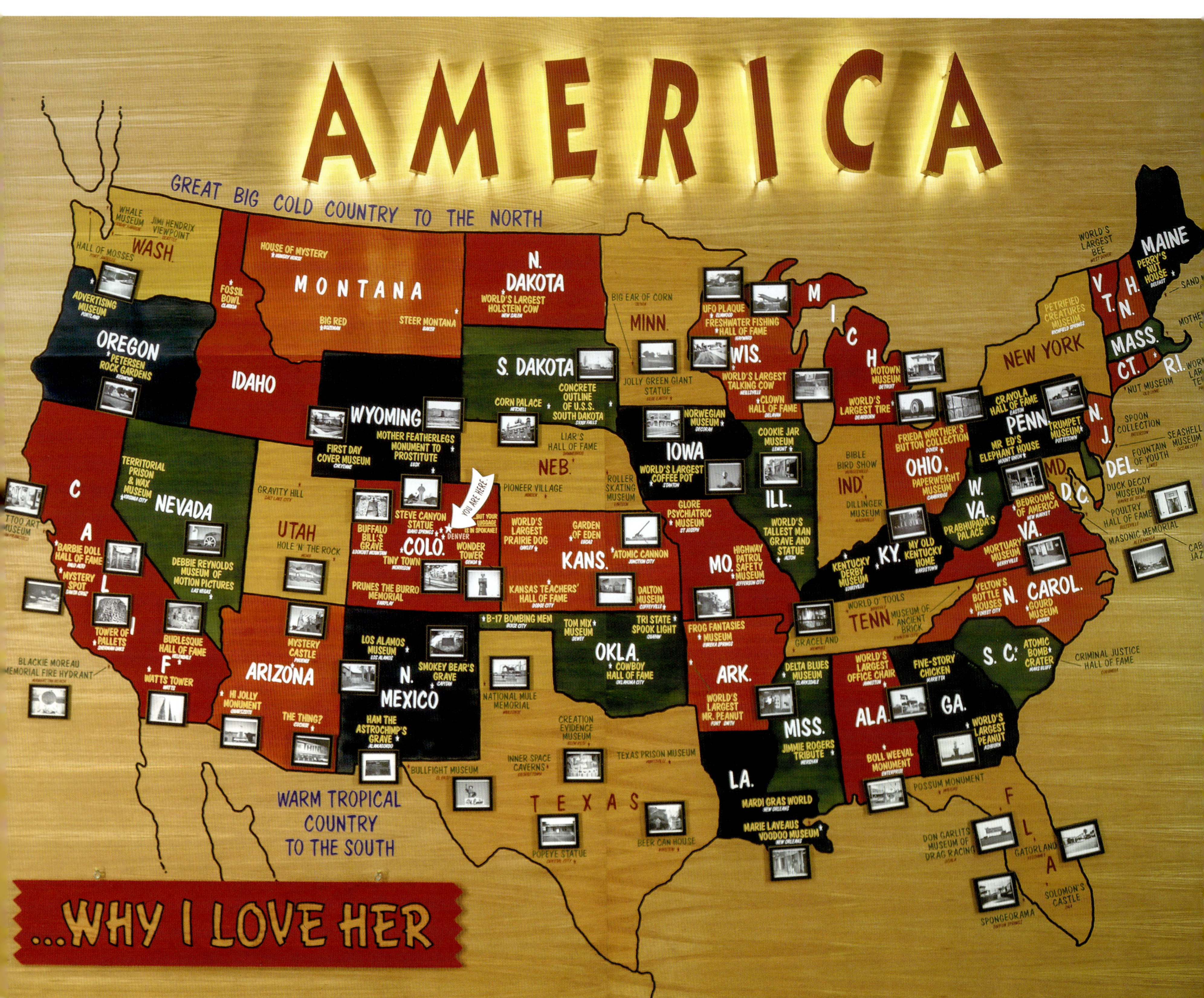

AMERICA
GREAT BIG COLD COUNTRY TO THE NORTH
WHALE MUSEUM
JIMI HENDRIX VIEWPOINT
HALL OF MOSSES
WASH.
ADVERTISING MUSEUM
OREGON
PETERSEN ROCK GARDENS
FOSSIL BOWL
IDAHO
HOUSE OF MYSTERY
MONTANA
BIG RED
STEER MONTANA
N. DAKOTA
WORLD'S LARGEST HOLSTEIN COW
BIG EAR OF CORN
MINN.
JOLLY GREEN GIANT STATUE
S. DAKOTA
CORN PALACE
CONCRETE OUTLINE OF U.S.S. SOUTH DAKOTA
WYOMING
MOTHER FEATHERLEGS MONUMENT TO PROSTITUTE
FIRST DAY COVER MUSEUM
LIAR'S HALL OF FAME
NEB.
PIONEER VILLAGE
ROLLER SKATING MUSEUM
UFO PLAQUE
FRESHWATER FISHING HALL OF FAME
WIS.
WORLD'S LARGEST TALKING COW
CLOWN HALL OF FAME
NORWEGIAN MUSEUM
IOWA
WORLD'S LARGEST COFFEE POT
COOKIE JAR MUSEUM
ILL.
WORLD'S TALLEST MAN GRAVE AND STATUE
M I C H
MOTOWN MUSEUM
WORLD'S LARGEST TIRE
BIBLE BIRD SHOW
IND.
DILLINGER MUSEUM
FRIEDA WARTHER'S BUTTON COLLECTION
OHIO
PAPERWEIGHT MUSEUM
NEW YORK
PETRIFIED CREATURES MUSEUM
CRAYOLA HALL OF FAME
PENN.
MR. ED'S ELEPHANT HOUSE
TRUMPET MUSEUM
N. J.
WORLD'S LARGEST BEE
MAINE
PERRY'S NUT HOUSE
V.T.
N.H.
MASS.
CT.
R.I.
NUT MUSEUM
SPOON COLLECTION
SEASHELL MUSEUM
FOUNTAIN OF YOUTH
DEL.
MD.
D.C.
DUCK DECOY MUSEUM
POULTRY HALL OF FAME
MASONIC MEMORIAL
W. VA.
PRABHUPADA'S PALACE
BEDROOMS OF AMERICA
VA.
MORTUARY MUSEUM
KENTUCKY DERBY MUSEUM
KY.
MY OLD KENTUCKY HOME
YELTON'S BOTTLE HOUSES
N. CAROL.
GOURD MUSEUM
WORLD O' TOOLS
TENN.
MUSEUM OF ANCIENT BRICK
GRACELAND
S. C.
ATOMIC BOMB CRATER
CRIMINAL JUSTICE HALL OF FAME
WORLD'S LARGEST OFFICE CHAIR
FIVE-STORY CHICKEN
ALA.
GA.
WORLD'S LARGEST PEANUT
BOLL WEEVIL MONUMENT
POSSUM MONUMENT
F L A
DON GARLITS MUSEUM OF DRAG RACING
GATORLAND
SOLOMON'S CASTLE
SPONGEORAMA
DELTA BLUES MUSEUM
MISS.
JIMMIE ROGERS TRIBUTE
LA.
MARDI GRAS WORLD
MARIE LAVEAUS VOODOO MUSEUM
GLORE PSYCHIATRIC MUSEUM
MO.
HIGHWAY PATROL SAFETY MUSEUM
FROG FANTASIES MUSEUM
ARK.
WORLD'S LARGEST MR. PEANUT
TOM MIX MUSEUM
TRI STATE SPOOK LIGHT
OKLA.
COWBOY HALL OF FAME
WORLD'S LARGEST PRAIRIE DOG
GARDEN OF EDEN
KANS.
ATOMIC CANNON
KANSAS TEACHERS' HALL OF FAME
DALTON MUSEUM
B-17 BOMBING MEM
NATIONAL MULE MEMORIAL
CREATION EVIDENCE MUSEUM
TEXAS PRISON MUSEUM
INNER SPACE CAVERNS
T E X A S
BULLFIGHT MUSEUM
POPEYE STATUE
BEER CAN HOUSE
STEVE CANYON STATUE
YOU ARE HERE.
BUT YOUR LUGGAGE IS IN SPOKANE!
DENVER
BUFFALO BILL'S GRAVE
COLO.
TINY TOWN
WONDER TOWER
PRUNES THE BURRO MEMORIAL
LOS ALAMOS MUSEUM
SMOKEY BEAR'S GRAVE
N. MEXICO
HAM THE ASTROCHIMP'S GRAVE
GRAVITY HILL
UTAH
HOLE 'N' THE ROCK
MYSTERY CASTLE
ARIZONA
HI JOLLY MONUMENT
THE THING?
TERRITORIAL PRISON & WAX MUSEUM
NEVADA
DEBBIE REYNOLDS MUSEUM OF MOTION PICTURES
C A L I F
BARBIE DOLL HALL OF FAME
MYSTERY SPOT
TOWER OF PALLETS
BURLESQUE HALL OF FAME
WATTS TOWER
BLACKIE MOREAU MEMORIAL FIRE HYDRANT
WARM TROPICAL COUNTRY TO THE SOUTH
...WHY I LOVE HER

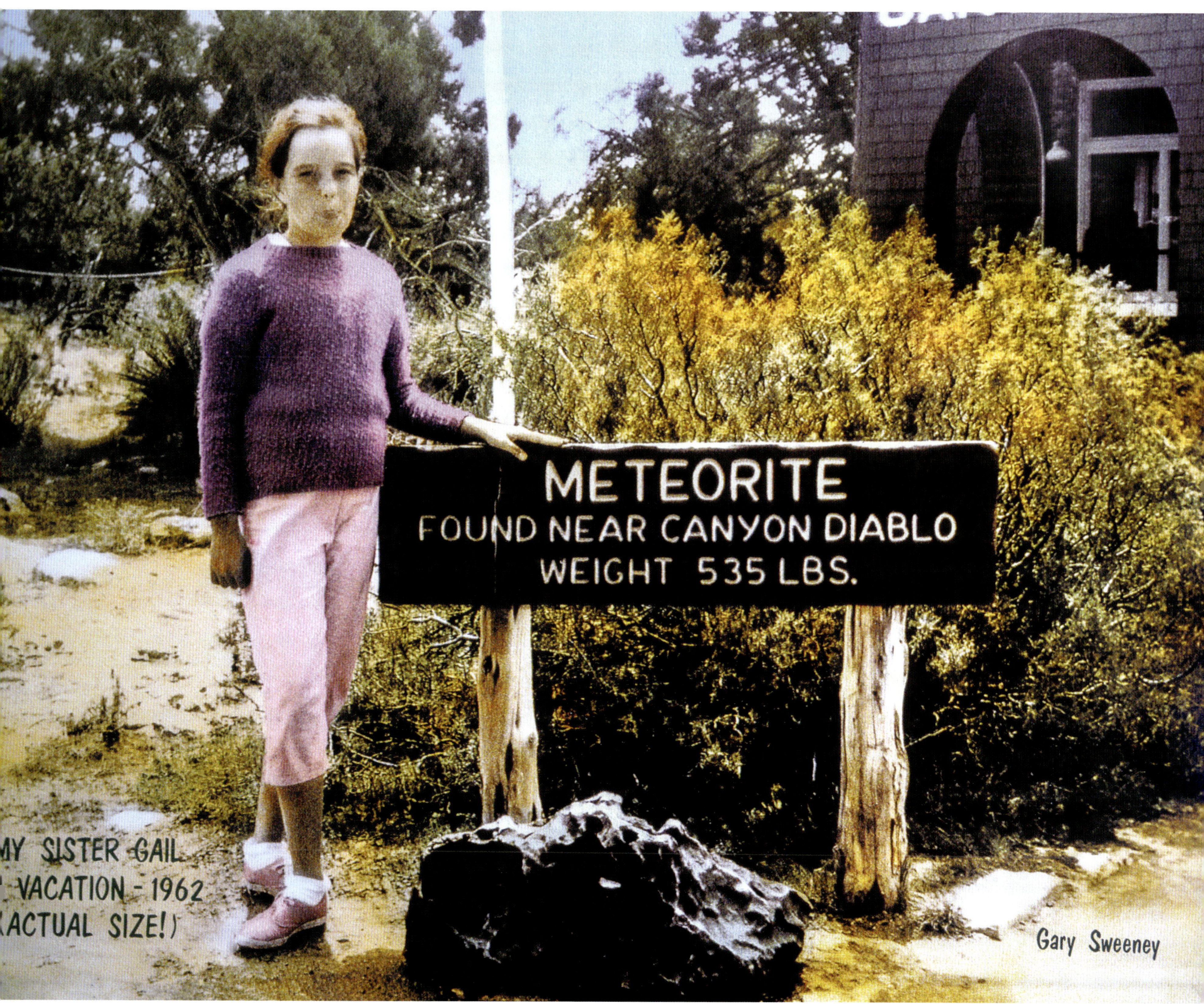
METEORITE
FOUND NEAR CANYON DIABLO
WEIGHT 535 LBS.
SISTER GAIL
VACATION - 1962
ACTUAL SIZE!)
Gary Sweeney

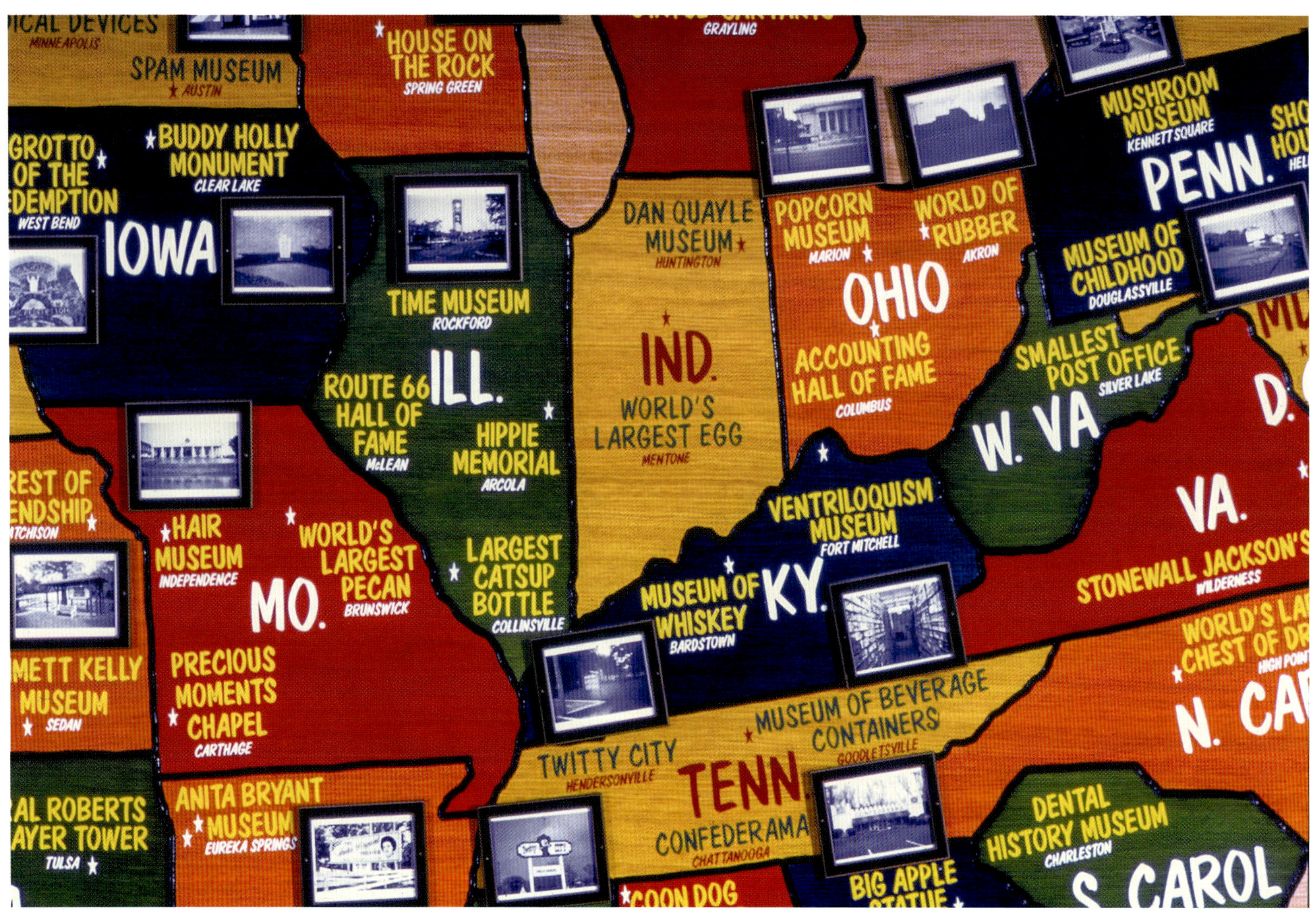

ABOVE & RIGHT » Details of northern wall

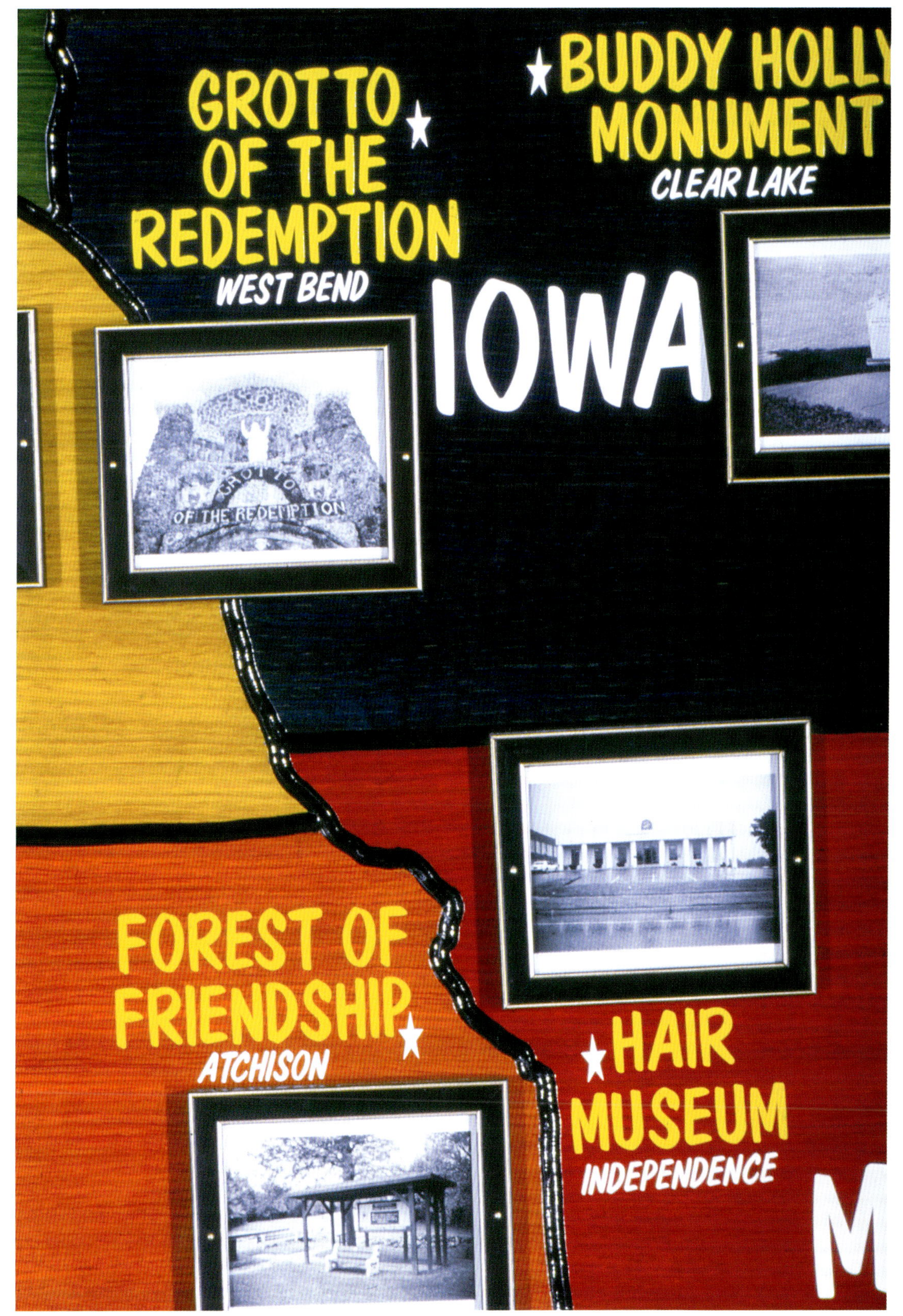
GROTTO OF THE REDEMPTION
WEST BEND
BUDDY HOLLY MONUMENT
CLEAR LAKE
IOWA
GROTTO OF THE REDEMPTION
FOREST OF FRIENDSHIP
ATCHISON
HAIR MUSEUM
INDEPENDENCE

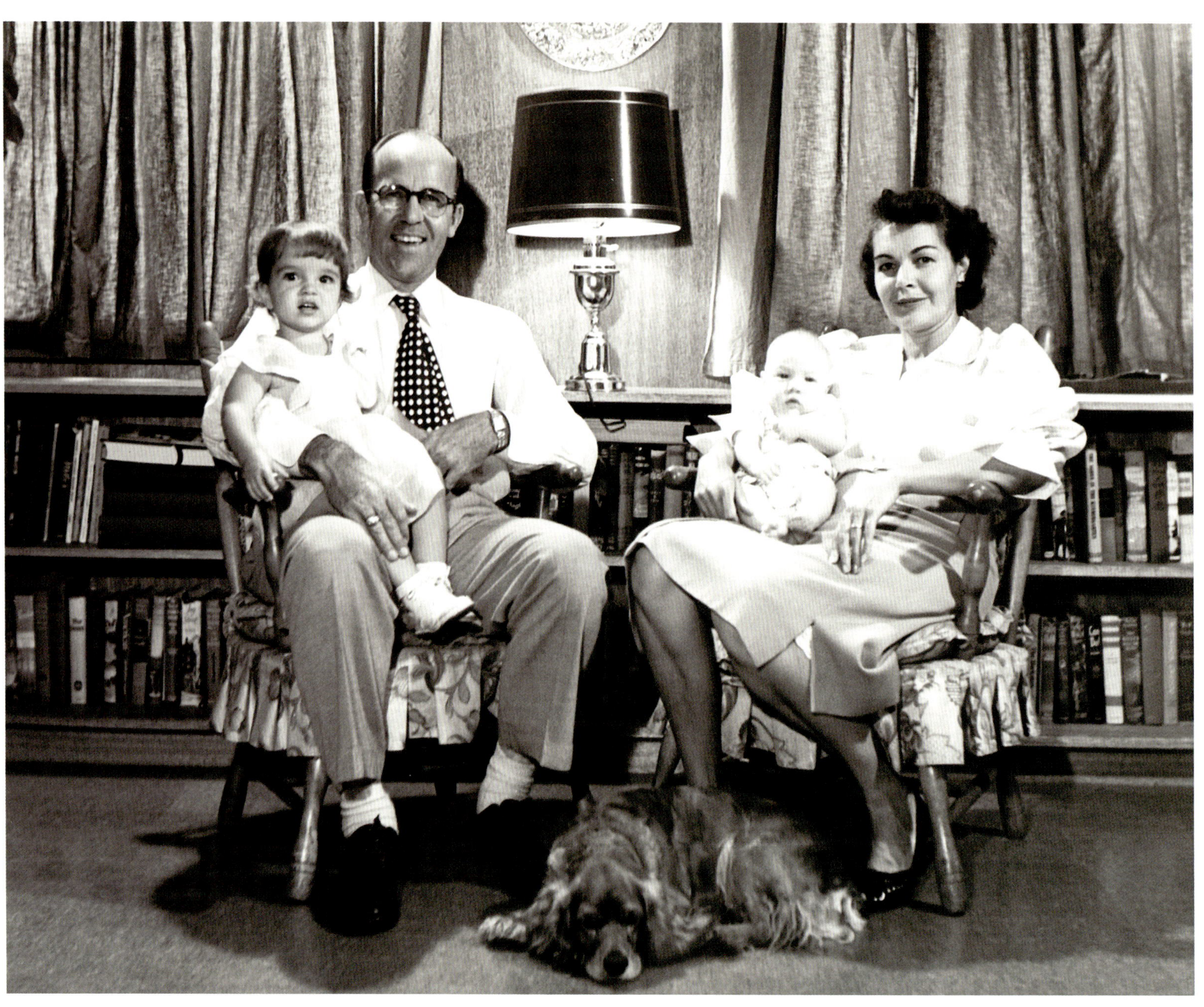

Happy Family

"Happy families are all alike; every unhappy family is unhappy in its own way," wrote Leo Tolstoy, but exactly how is the question on everyone's mind. [19]

"We had a typical middle-class upbringing," said Gary. "There were two kids and a dog and a stay-at-home mom with a grandmother who lived there. The only difference was that my father took hundreds of photographs of the first day of school and Christmas and every big event of our lives." [20]

After returning from WWII, Mike photographed crime scenes for the Los Angeles Police Department. For a hobby, he turned his lens towards his family. "The camera is the ideal arm of consciousness in its acquisitive mood," wrote Susan Sontag. "Photographs furnish evidence." Gary's father kept most of his pictures in his darkroom, which preserved the prints' condition. He saved every newspaper article and dated every photo, creating a meticulous family archive that details the life of his family.

During the 1950-60s, photography's technological innovations allowed it to become increasingly accessible and affordable. "Photography has become almost as widely practiced an amusement as sex and dancing—which means that, like every mass art form, photography is not practiced by most people as an art," wrote Sontag in 1973. "It is mainly a social rite, a defense against anxiety, and a tool of power." [21] This was also the post WWII era of consumption—each click of the shutter was like a new possession: "The camera is the ideal arm of consciousness in its acquisitive mood." [22]

"My father was definitely on the hoarder spectrum, but in an organized way," said Gary, referring to the towering stacks of albums that his father kept stashed away in his darkroom. The huge collection of pictures became his legacy, the remnants of his mind's eye, temporarily withstanding time's imminent erasure.

Mike maintained a compulsive, habitual practice of photographing his family, capturing moments, documenting his deep appreciation for his children. He and his wife, Anita, were older parents who had tried for many years to have a family—Anita was 38 when she had Gary's older sister, Gail.

"Cameras go with families ... Through photographs, each family constructs a portrait-chronicle of itself—a portable kit of images that bears witness to its connectedness." [23]

Having a photographer in the family requires a continued submission to the lens, but the payoff is a wealthy cache of recorded moments that might otherwise be forgotten.

"I have a lot of friends and neighbors who say the only photographs they have of their childhood are the ones taken by my dad," said Gary.

The Sweeney family's "portrait-chronicle" documents holidays, pets, and special events. There are photographic portraits of every family member including cousins and grandparents. Gary and Gail sit for their portraits dressed in costumes.

"He had a seamless grey blanket that he'd use as a backdrop and we'd get dressed up to pose. It was so much a part of our lives that it seemed normal," said Gary.

Sometimes Mike even designed sets specifically for their portrait sittings. Gary is dressed in cowboy suits, Western shirts, and a Daniel Boone costume (his mother told him later that it could be the hottest day and he'd still have that hat on). Gail poses in a flouncy dress set inside a paper cutout of a heart for Valentine's Day. Cole's phrase, "invented scenarios" suggests how the photographer's imagination frames an image.[24] These perfected, idealized versions of life contrast with the inescapable flaws of real life.

Portraiture has always been a process of meticulous curation; it is a heady task to select a representative image. And the image selection process may also reveal what a person sees in themselves and what remains unconscious. This process continues in social media. The selected images, however perfected, tell an incomplete narrative that reinforces certain memories while erasing others. Yet to comprehensively document life would be an insurmountable task, like a Borgesian map.

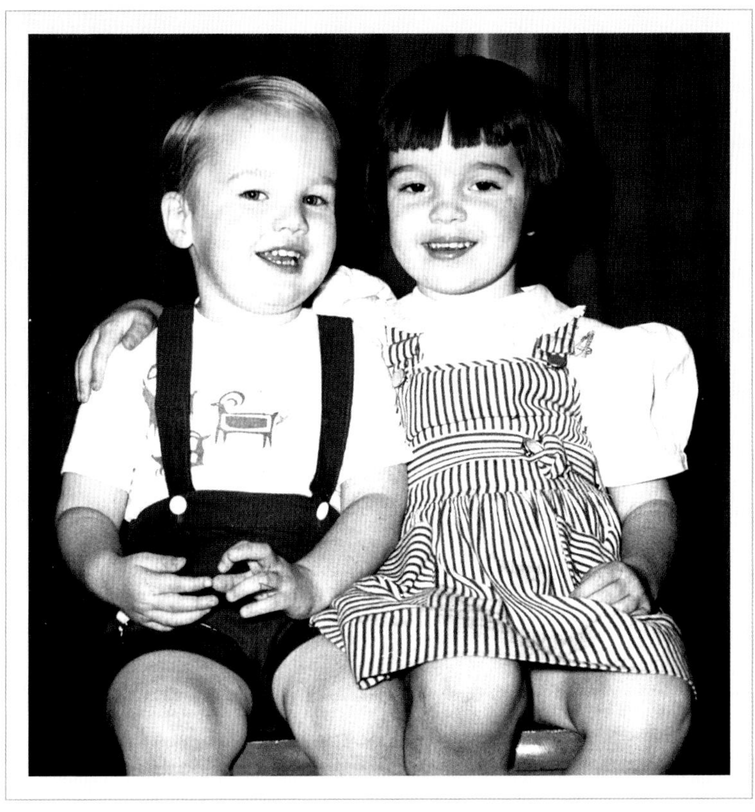
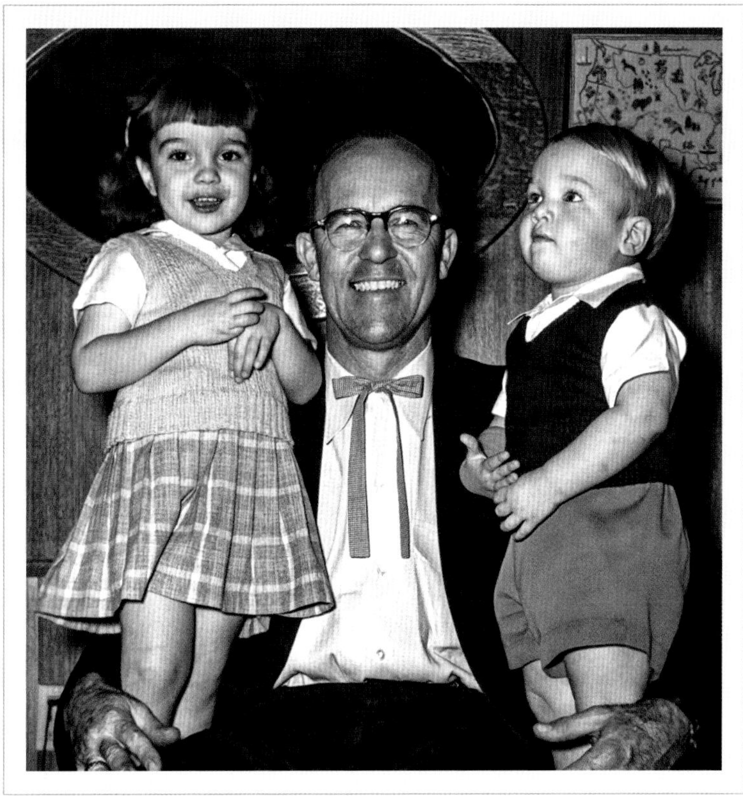
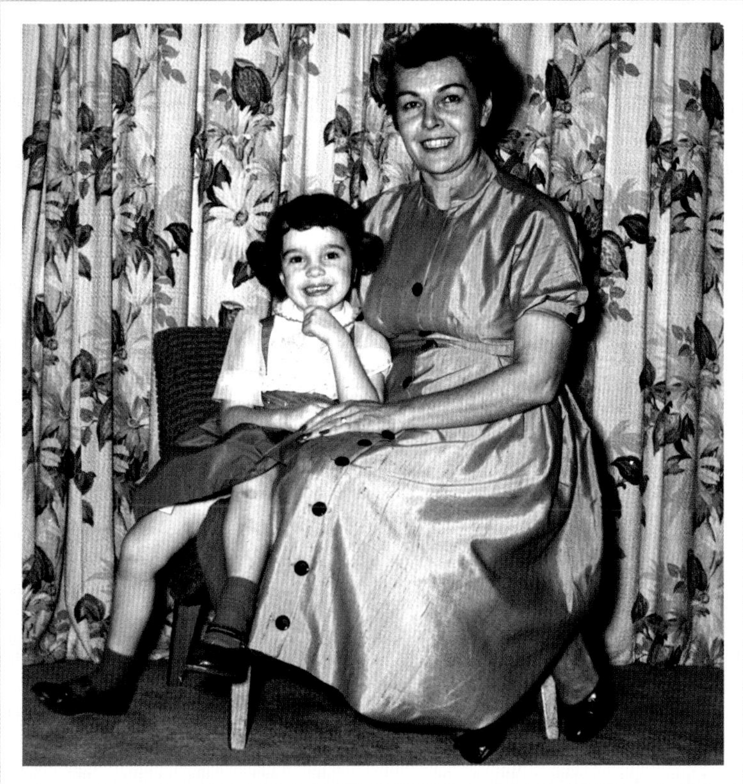
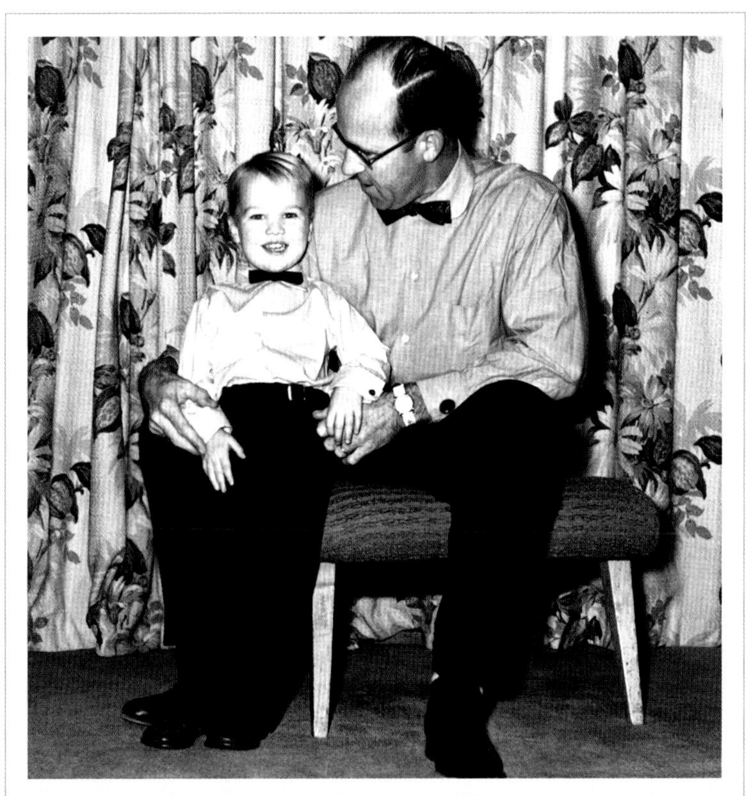

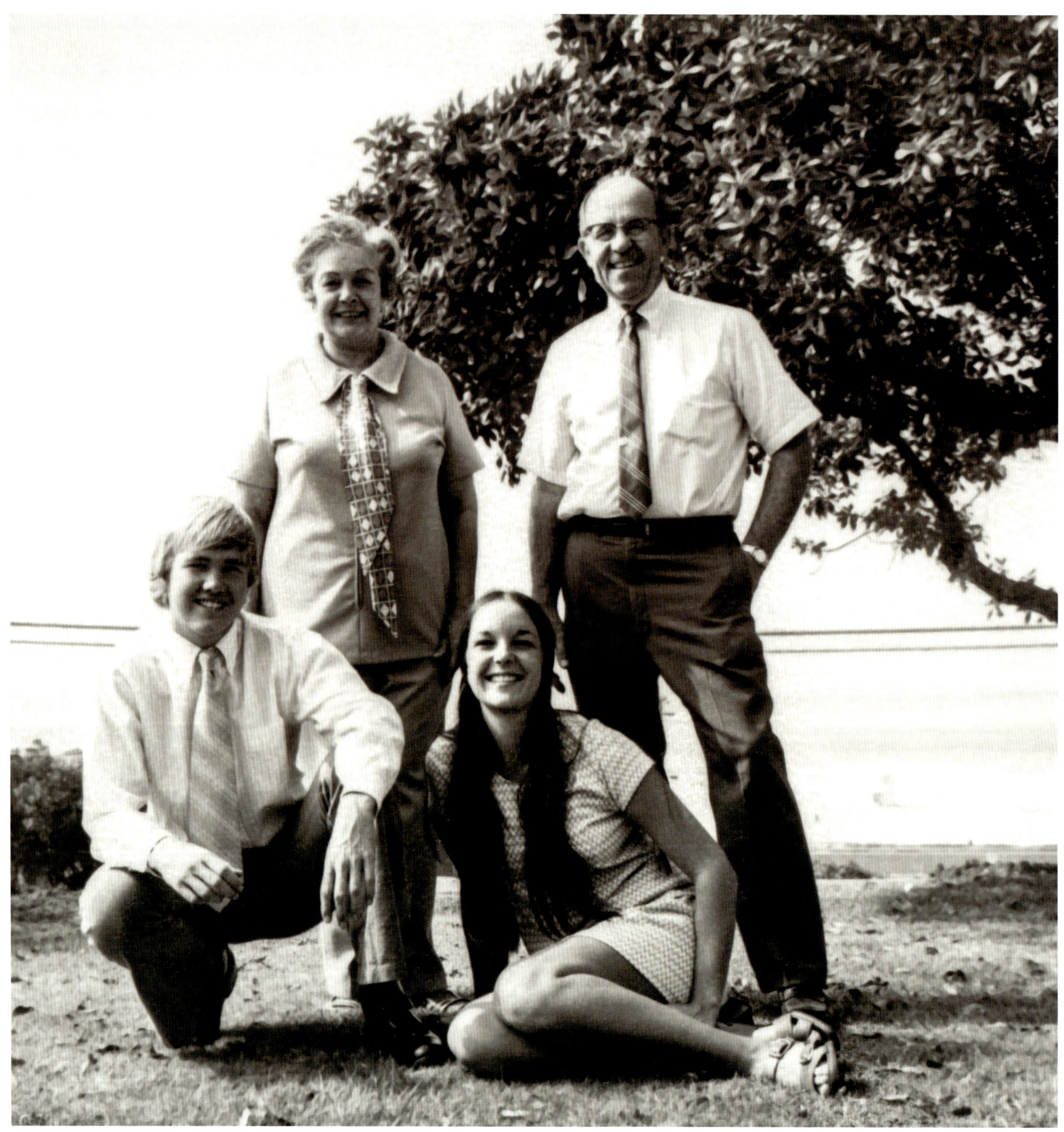

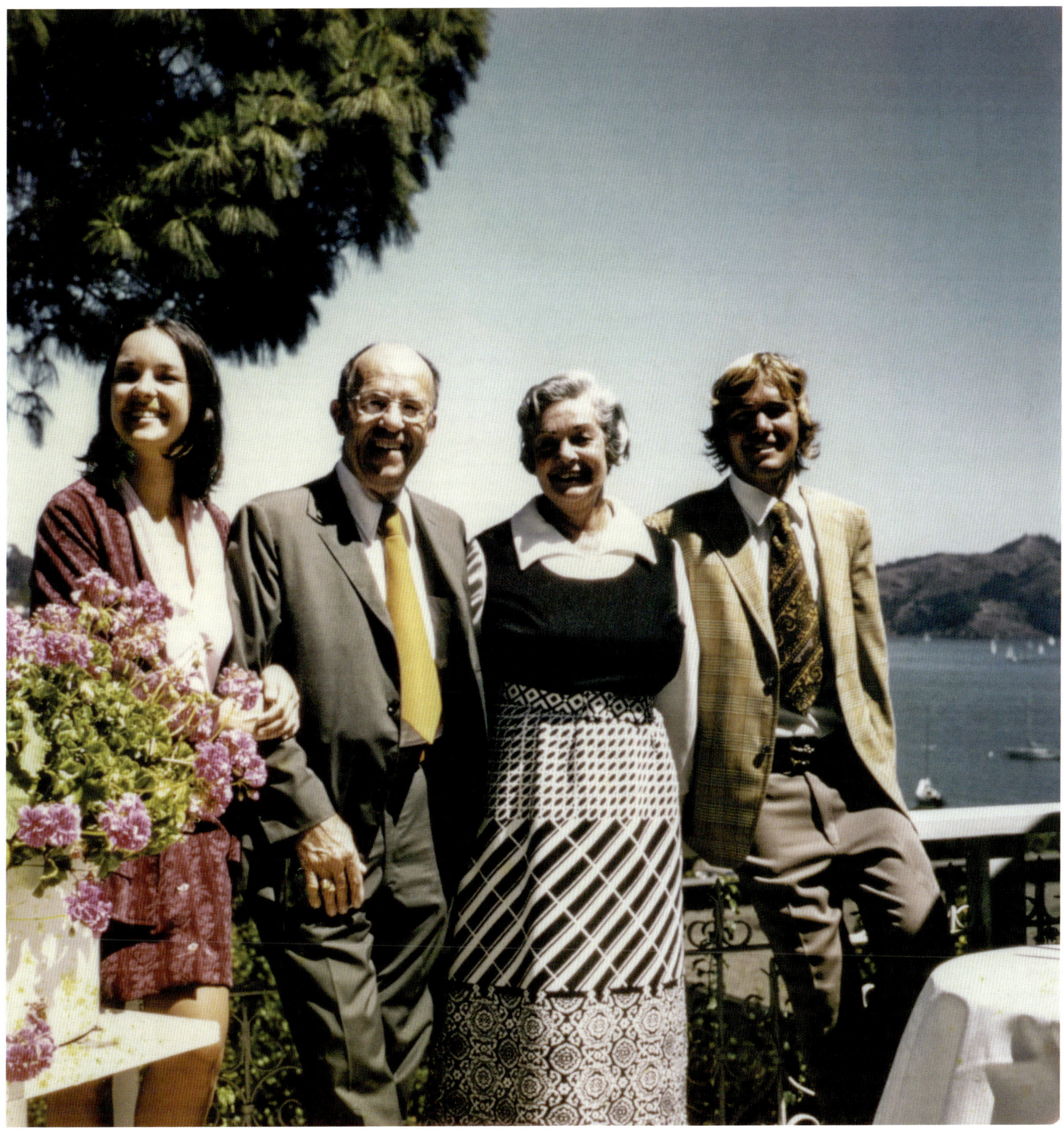

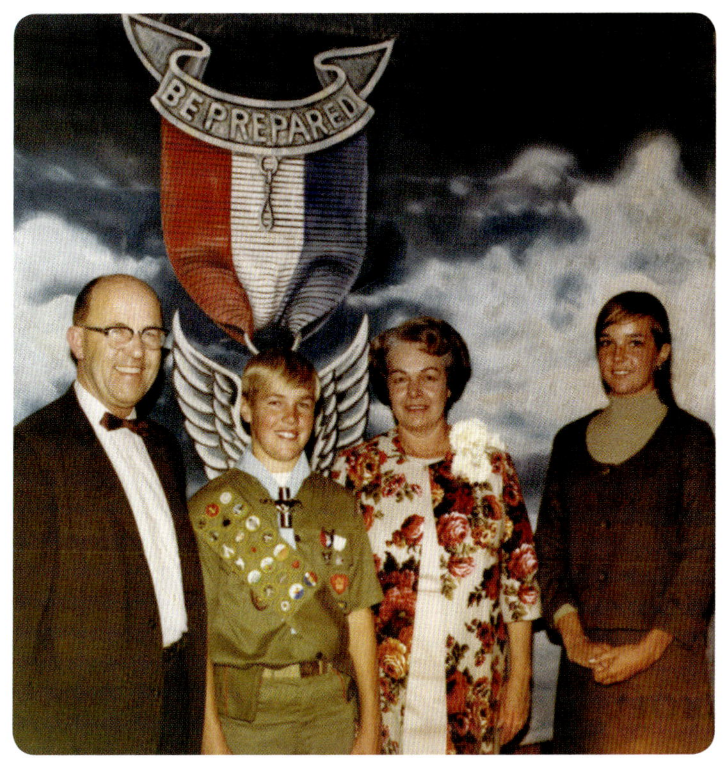
BE PREPARED

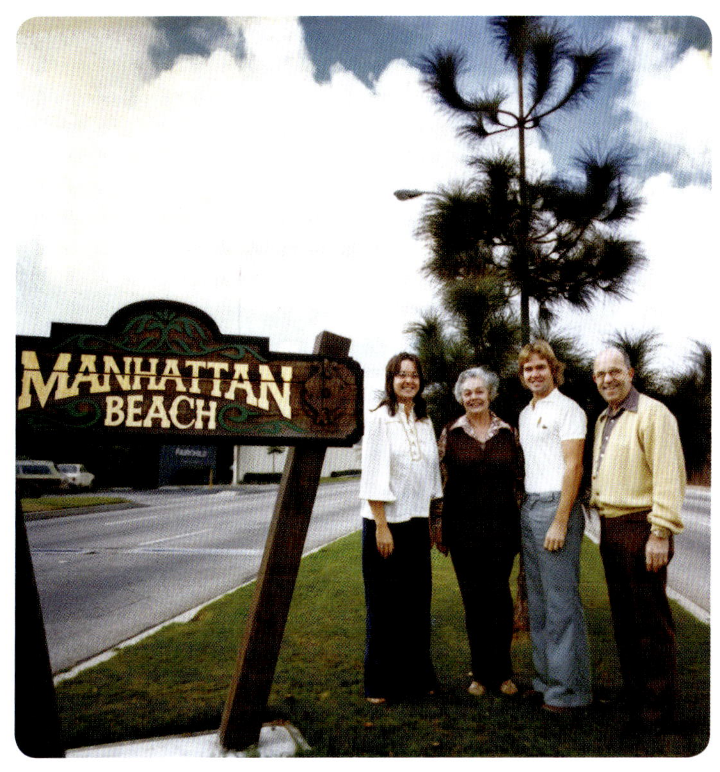
MANHATTAN
BEACH

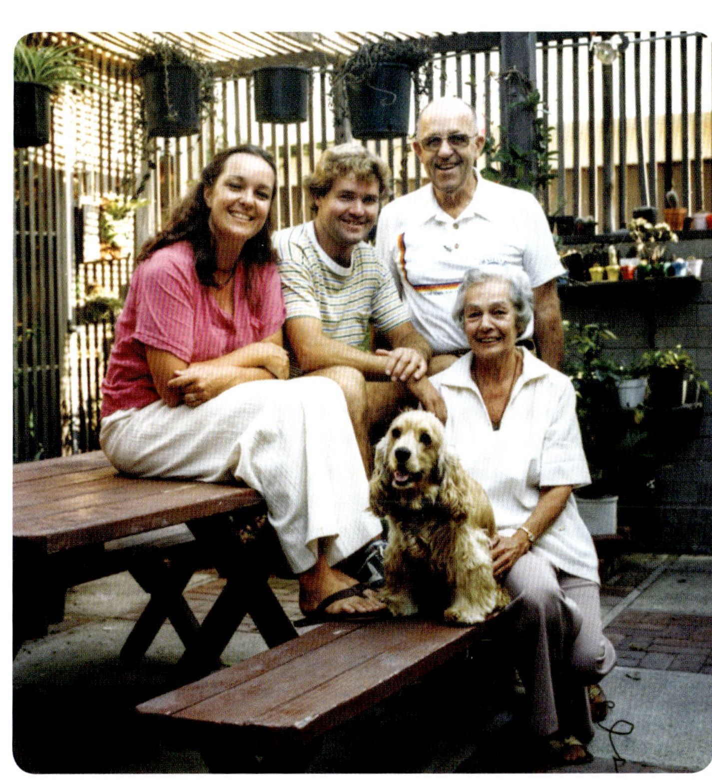

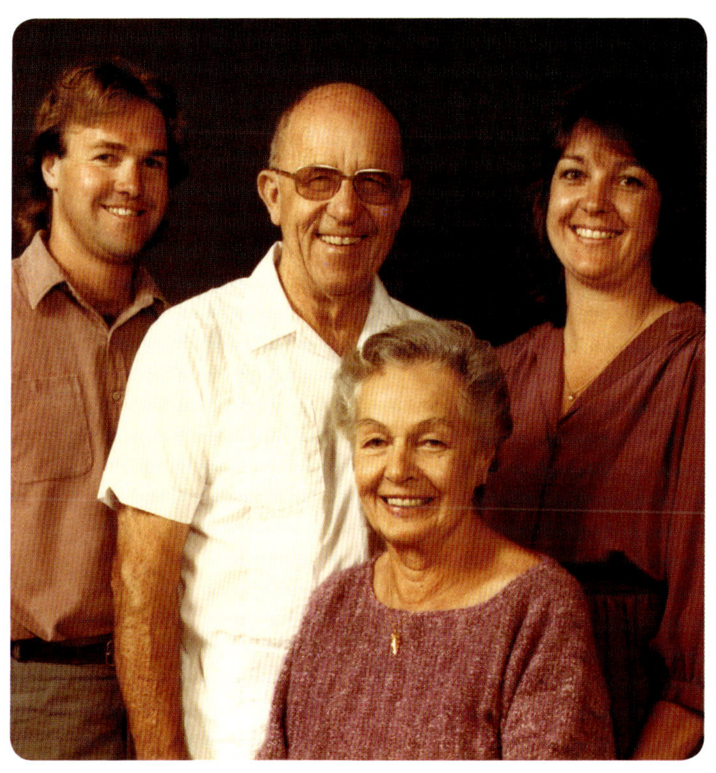

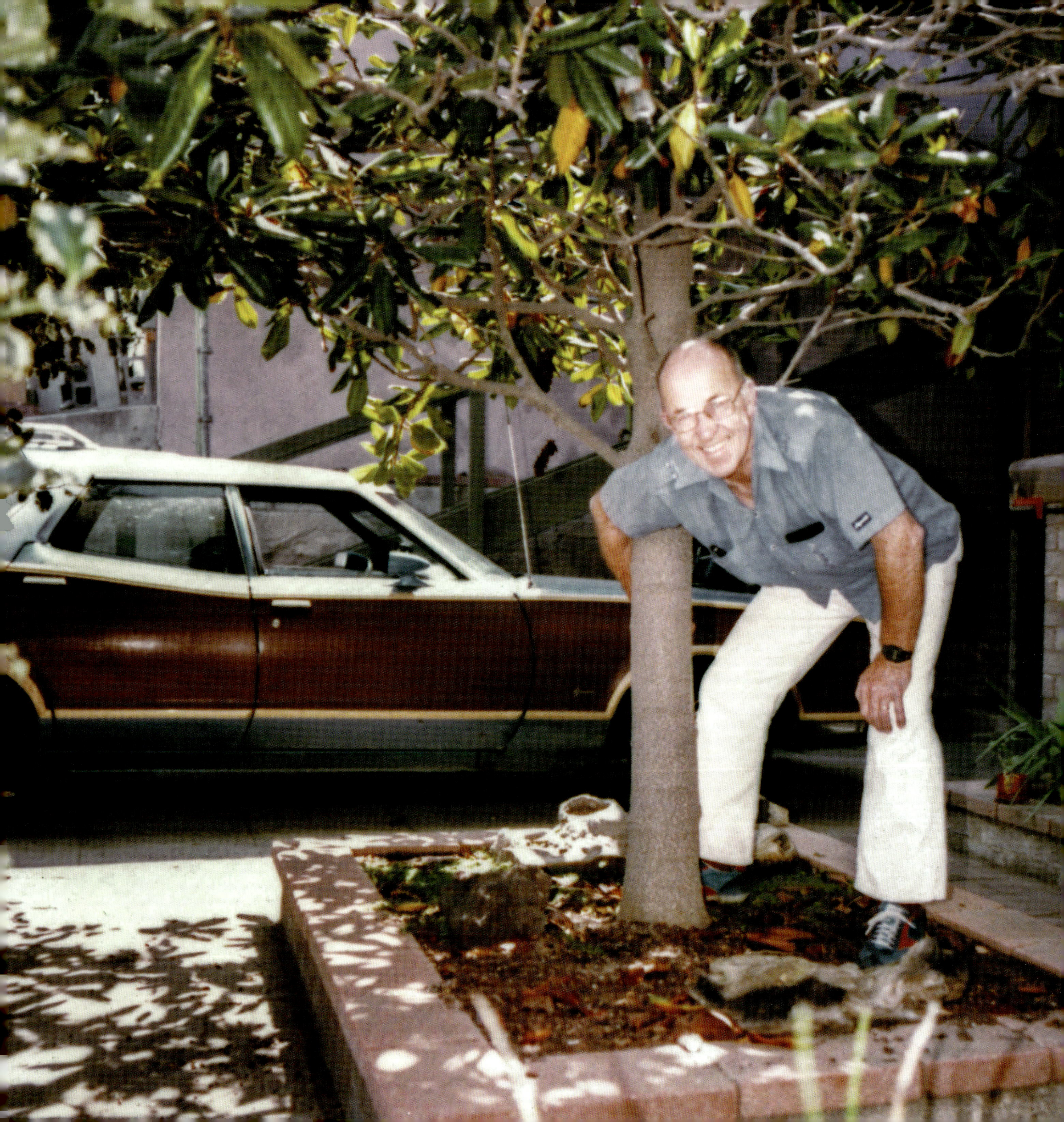

Time

Mike had multiple "invented scenarios" that he repeated throughout the years. Every Christmas, the extended family posed together in the same order, a vertical line of beaming white faces that form a 20th-century totem pole (the metal step stool Mike used to achieve the vertical order is only slightly visible in some images). His family also posed for a Christmas card picture every year. Christmas cards and portraits bring an awareness to their subjects, a consciousness that they are being recorded for posterity.

Like penciled lines on the door frame that mark a child's growth, these customs are touchstones, rituals to return to that provide a sense of comfort and meaning. Observing customs takes a certain amount of diligence and with this comes the reward of predictability and reliability, staving off the inevitable changes that come with time.

The photographer Nicholas Nixon also created a series of images that involved the careful recording of time. In 1975, Nixon began photographing his wife (Bebe) and her three sisters, and he has taken a photograph of them every year since. Posing in the same order—Heather, Mimi, Bebe, and Laurie—the sisters' faces wear the passage of time. Even as the women may be strangers to the viewer, the shared progression of their aging creates a captivating intimacy. There is something gracious and generous about these shared images, as if, through the photos, the sisters are sacrificing their individuality to the service of a larger narrative, the subject of time.

With his photos, Gary provides a similar offering. The family's repetitive customs—Gary and his sister posing with their birthday cakes, on the first day of school, and in their Halloween costumes—prompt the viewer's own childhood memories.

LEFT » *My father was gifted a magnolia tree from the Grandview Elementary School PTA for his retirement. For decades, it was the most gorgeous beautiful tree, blossoming and thriving, but six months before we sold the house, it died.*

The Sweeneys' family photos are informal versions of "timed photographic studies" that William Christenberry took of his childhood landscape in rural Alabama.[25] Throughout his life, Christenberry returned again and again to photograph the same building. "Time is photography's illusion. Almost every photograph appears instantaneous. But of course, there's no such thing as instantaneous: all fragments of time have a length ... Between one exposure and the next, time passes, life goes on and the artist reencounters his or her altered subject."[26]

Seen together side by side, the years cascade by in an exposition of time's tricks. Between these multiple frozen moments time has flown; time has vanished. Time has also changed people, very slowly, but the gaps in between reveal the changes. These larger events and traditions bookend the more mundane parts of life, the familiar rituals of the day, our habitual tendencies. From Christmas to summer, we are constantly taunted out of the present moment, getting lost in the magic of future's mirage.

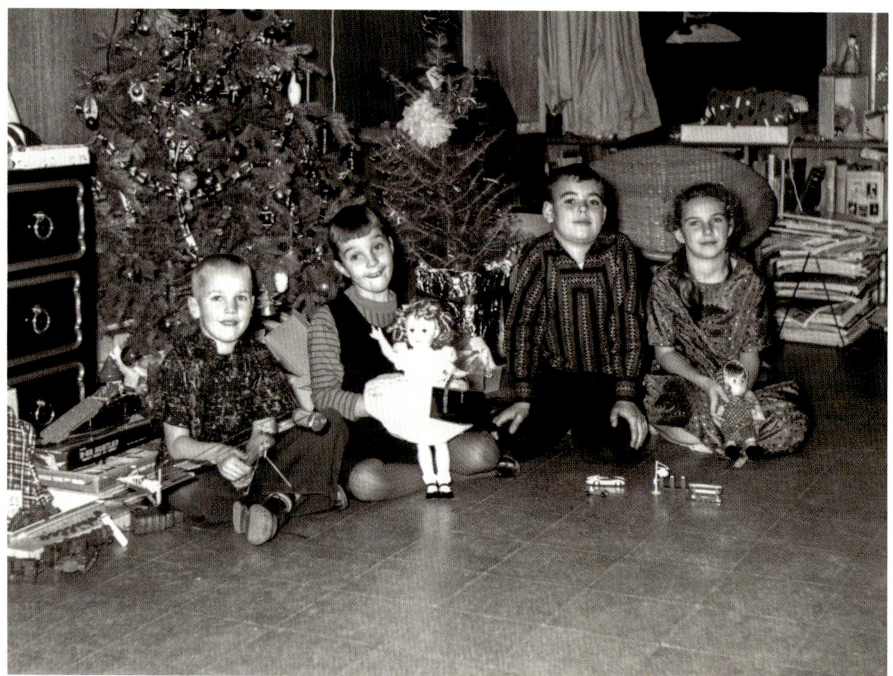

» *Needless to say, Christmas was when the camera came out.*

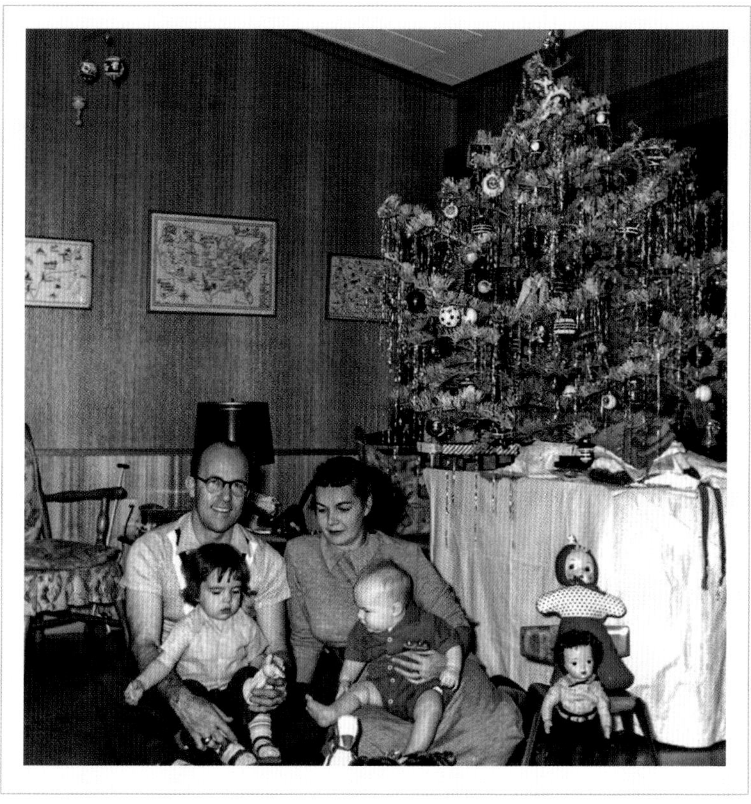

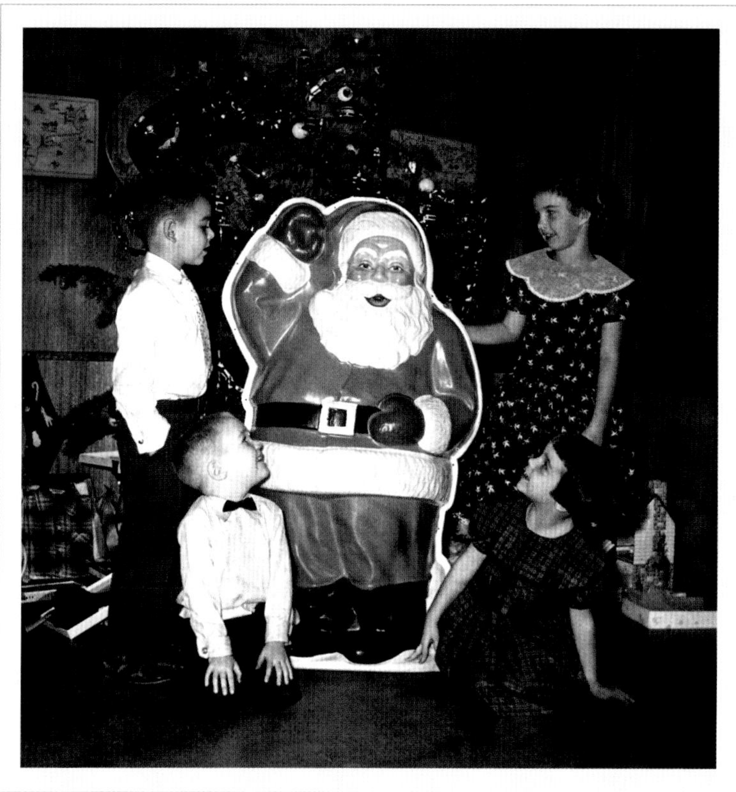

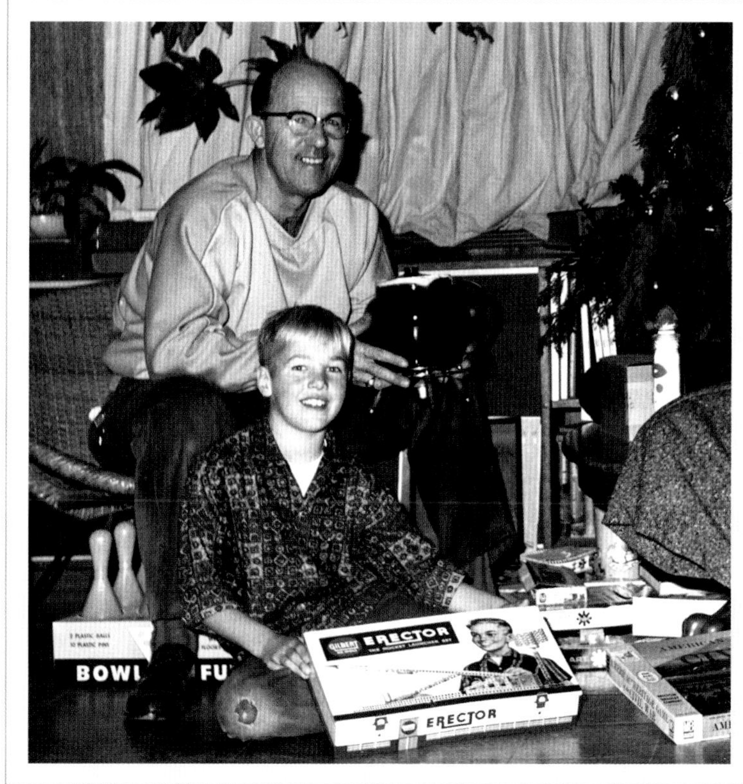
ERECTOR
ERECTOR

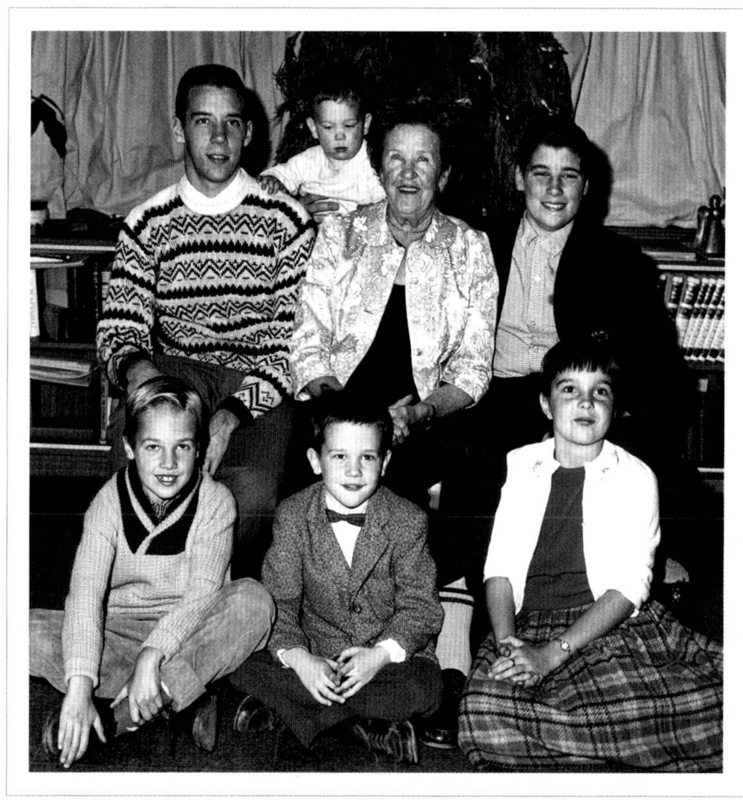

RIGHT » *Every year my father created our family portrait and made our family Christmas cards.*

FAR RIGHT » *And then there was also the obligatory four cousins Christmas day photograph*

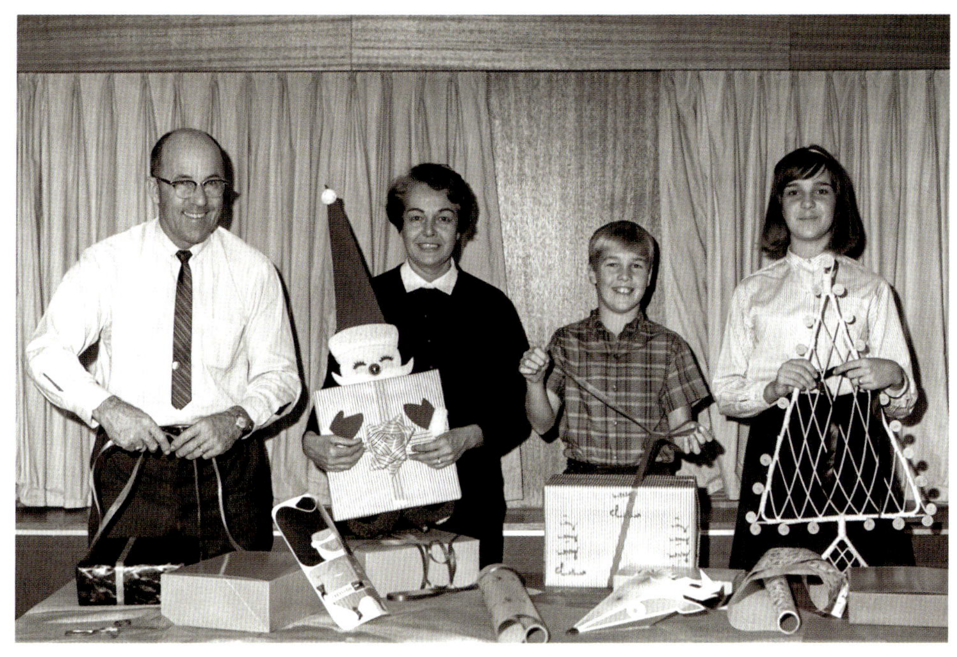

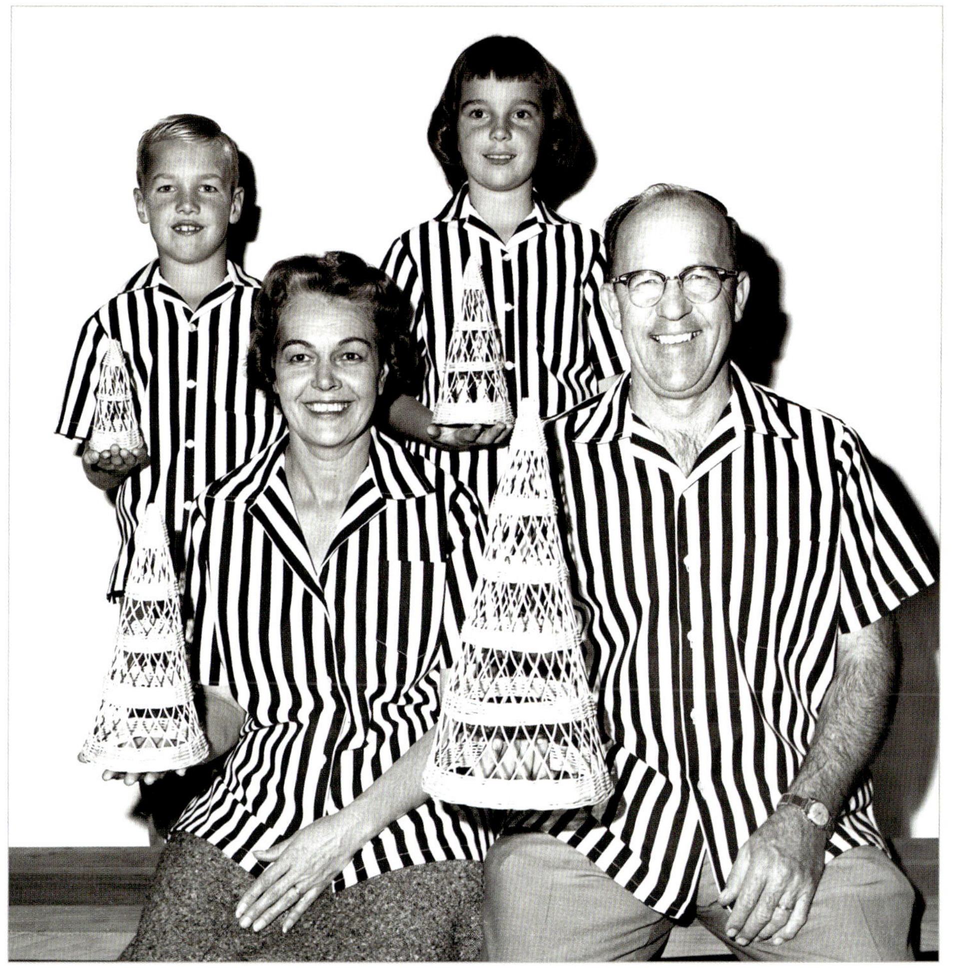

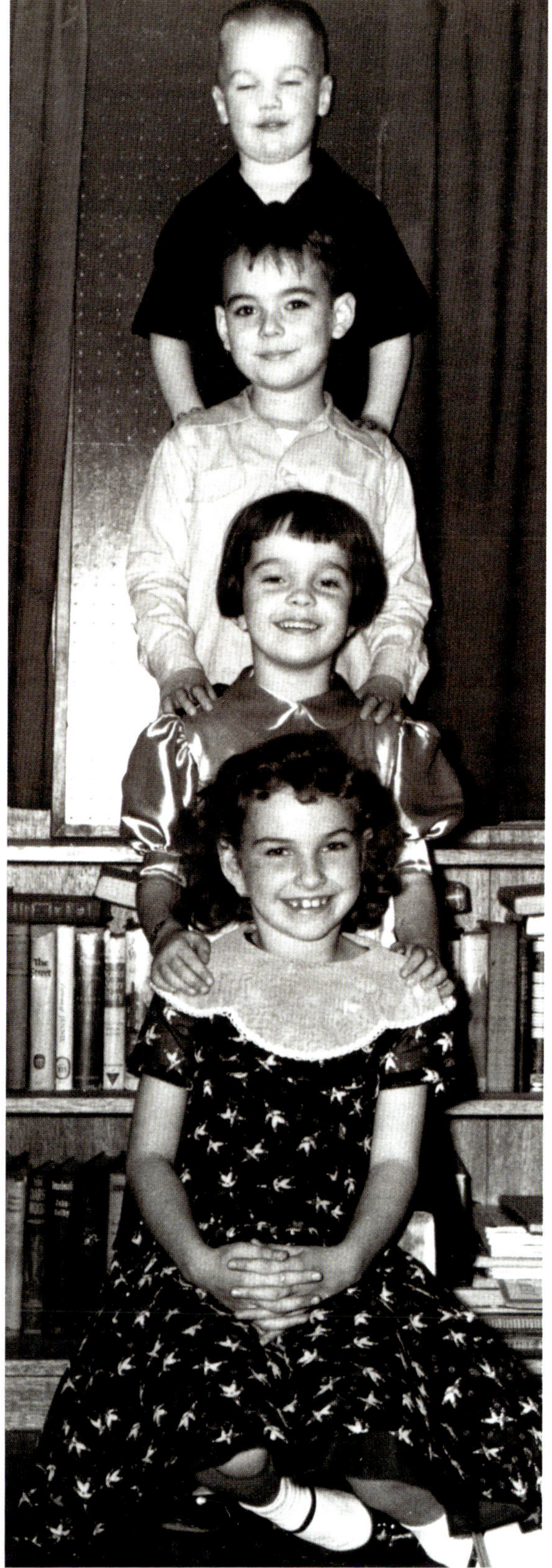

Every year, even into adulthood, the four cousins would line up by order of height for our family Christmas photo. There were some surprising changes throughout the years.

TOP LEFT » 1966

TOP RIGHT » 1967

BOTTOM LEFT » 1968

BOTTOM RIGHT » 1970

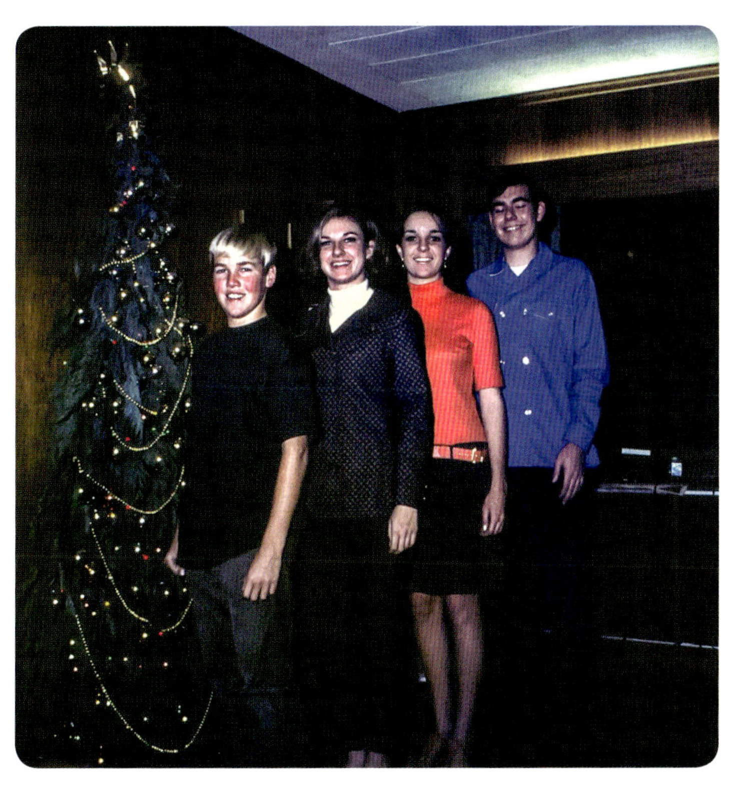

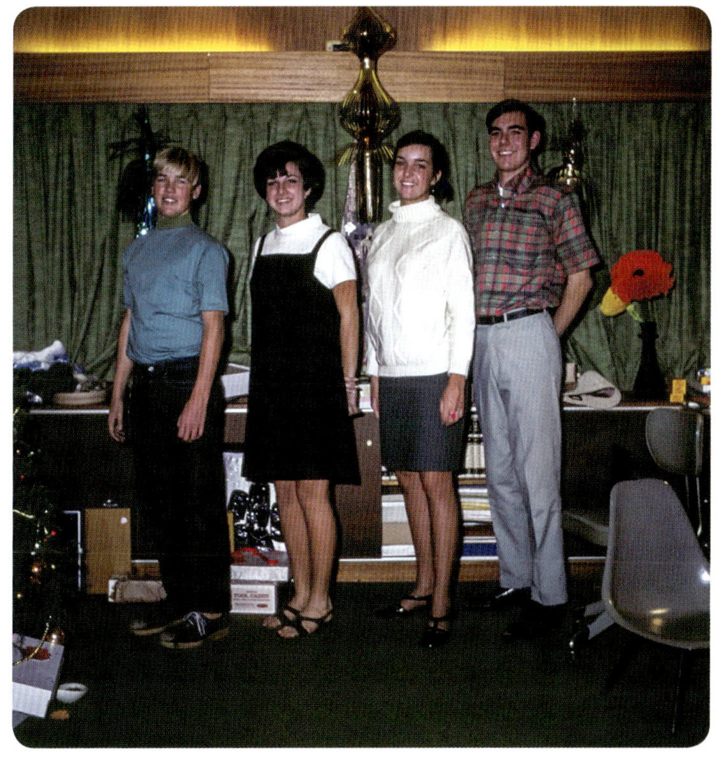

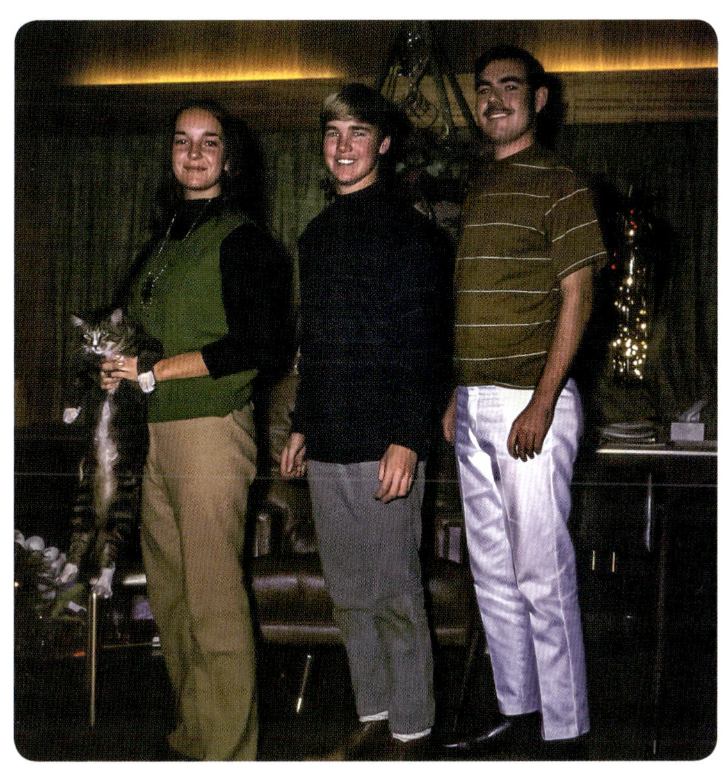

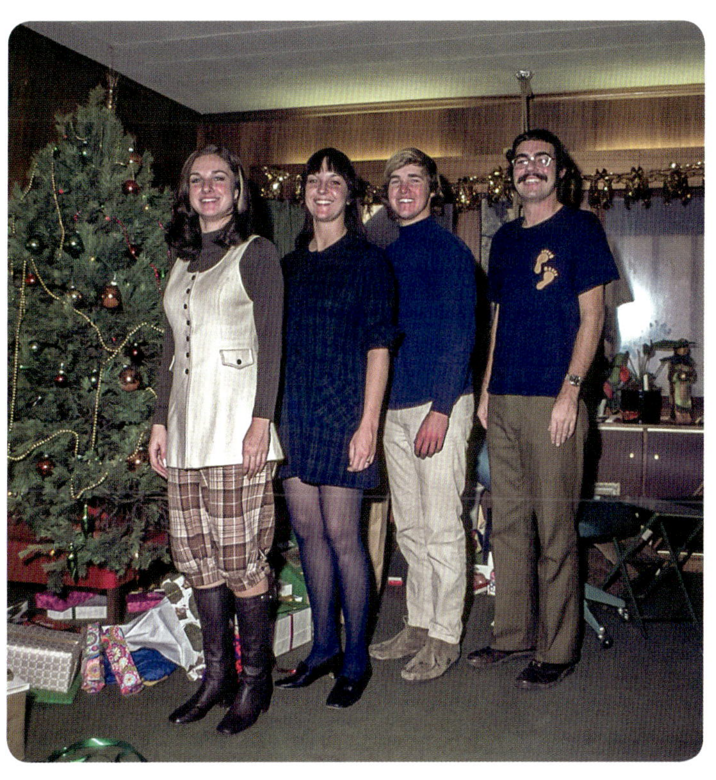

Rising Tides, Neil Fauerso

1 Michel Houellebcq, *Submission* (New York, Farrar, Straus and Giroux, 2105)

2 Kevin Cody, "Ultrafication Manhattan Beach: the impact of ultra wealth on the once laid back beach town," *Easy Reader News,* June 30, 2016, https://easyreadernews.com/ultrafication-manhattan-beach-impact-ultra-wealth/

Sunset on Manhattan Beach, Wendy Weil Atwell

1 Megan Barnes, "70 Years, A Million Memories, One Home," *Daily Breeze,* February 1, 2016, A1.

2 Geoff Dyer, "The Mysteries of Our Family Snapshots," *New York Times Magazine,* January 3, 2017, https://www.nytimes.com/2017/01/03/magazine/the-mysteries-of-our-family-snapshots.html.

3 Morgan Neville, *The Cool School: Story of the Ferus Art Gallery.* Digital Documentary Film, written by Morgan Neville and Kristine McKenna (2007; Los Angeles: Tremelo Productions, 2007.) Retrieved from https://www.amazon.com.

4 All historical information was sourced from Judson Grenier: "A Manhattan Beach Historical Series Publication," No. 3, 1975, Manhattan Beach Historical Society, http://manhattanbeachhistorical.org/history/ (accessed July 25, 2017), and from John Post and Manhattan Beach Historical Society, *Manhattan Beach Centennial 1912-2012* (Hermosa Beach, California: Anthro-Graphics, 2012).

5 Ken Little, "Gary Sweeney: Imagining Words," in *Gary Sweeney: A Forty-Year Overview,* (San Antonio: Blue Star Contemporary, 2013), 14.

6 Gary Sweeney, *Gary Sweeney: A Forty-Year Overview,* 15.

7 Alexandra Schwartz, "Second City: Ed Ruscha and the Reception of Los Angeles Pop," *October,* Winter, No. 111 (2005): 25.

8 The first mention of Los Angeles as a "second city" was mentioned by L.A. critic Jules Langsner in "Art Centers, Los Angeles, America's Second Art City," *Art in America,* April, 1963 and later in Barbara Rose, "Los Angeles: The Second City," *Art in America* 54, January- February 1966, 110-115. Schwartz, "Second City," 33-34, 40.

9 Schwartz, "Second City," 32.

10 Alexandra Schwartz, "Second City: Ed Ruscha and the Reception of Los Angeles Pop," *October,* Winter, No. 111 (2005): 25.

11 Neville, Morgan, *Cool School.* Written by Morgan Neville and Kristine McKenna (2007; City: Tremelo Productions, 2007.) Digital Documentary Film.

12 Schwartz, Alexandra. *Ed Ruscha's Los Angeles* (Cambridge: MIT Press, 2010), 120.

13 Reyner Banham, *Los Angeles: The Architecture of Four Ecologies* (Berkeley: University of California Press, 1971), 131.

14 Teju Cole, "The Superhero Photographs of the Black Lives Matter Movement," *New York Times Magazine,* July 26, 2016. https://www.nytimes.com/2016/07/31/magazine/thesuperhero-photographs-of-the-black-lives-matter-movement.html.

15 Thomas Pynchon, *Vineland,* (New York: Penguin Books, 1990), 111.

16 Catherine Walworth, *Gary Sweeney: A Forty-Year Overview*, 11.

17 Michael Paglia, "Denver Years: 1982-1994," *Gary Sweeney: A Forty-Year Overview*, 8.

18 Barnes, "70 Years," A1.

19 Leo Tolstoy, *Anna Karenina,* (Norwalk: The Easton Press), 1.

20 Michael Hixon, "Photographic Memories," *The Beach Reporter,* January 28, 2016, 26.

21 Susan Sontag, *On Photography* (New York: Farrar, Straus and Giroux, 1973), 4.

22 Sontag, *On Photography,* 4.

23 Sontag, *On Photography,* 8-9.

24 Teju Cole, "Getting Others Right," *New York Times Magazine,* June 13, 2017, https://www.nytimes.com/2017/06/13/magazine/getting-others-right.html.

25 Teju Cole, "The Image of Time," *New York Times Magazine,* January 31, 2017, https://www.nytimes.com/2017/01/31/magazine/the-image-of-time.html.

26 Cole, "The Image of Time."

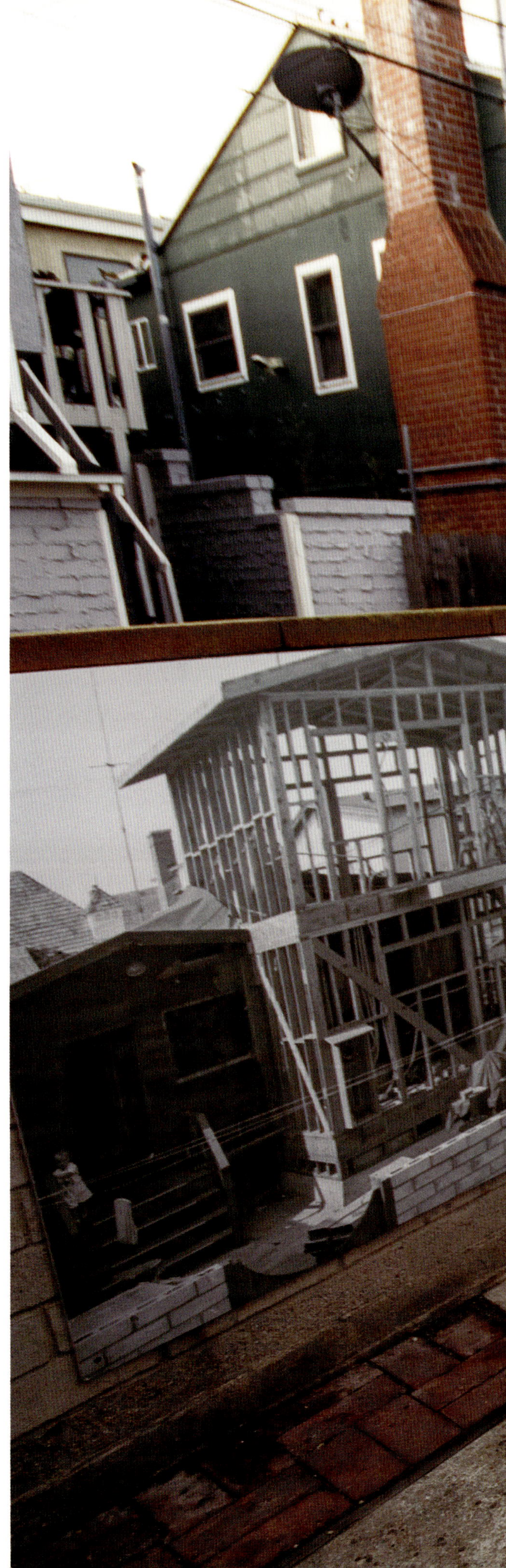

RIGHT » View of the backyard in 2016, with photo of Mike Sweeney placed in the exact spot where he was standing for the photo taken in 1996, with the plumeria tree behind him.

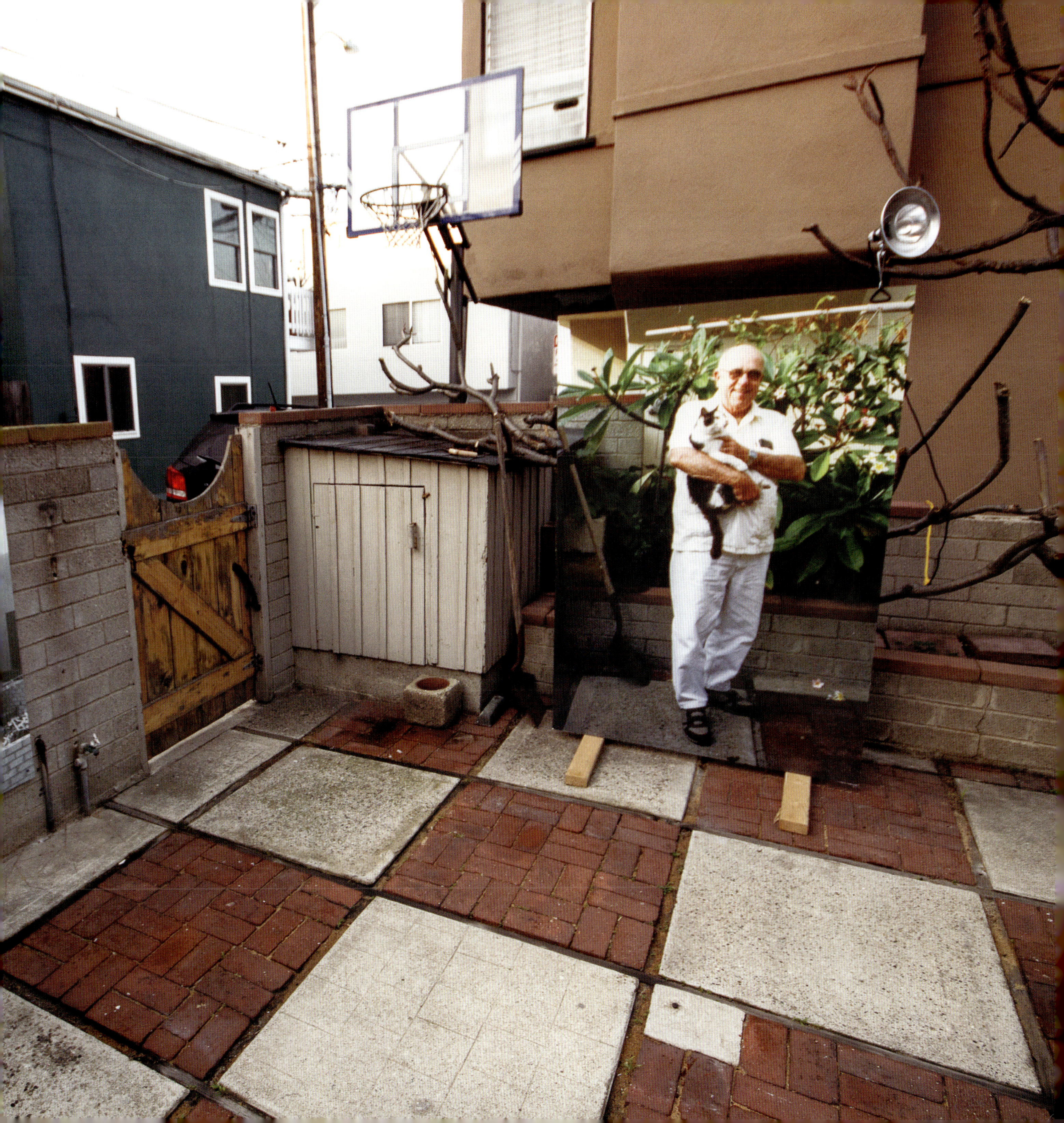

The only known photo of both sides of the Sweeney family, taken around 1961 (not shown: Cousin Mark Johnson)

TOP ROW »

Everett Felsing / Vera Gordon / Larry Johnson / Anita Sweeney / Arthur Johnson / Kay Johnson / Peter Johnson

CENTER ROW »

Eric Johnson / Estelle Felsing / Dixie Brock (family friend) / Maggie Sweeney / Mike Sweeney

BOTTOM ROW »

Gail Sweeney / Gary Sweeney / Ron Felsing / Barbara Felsing

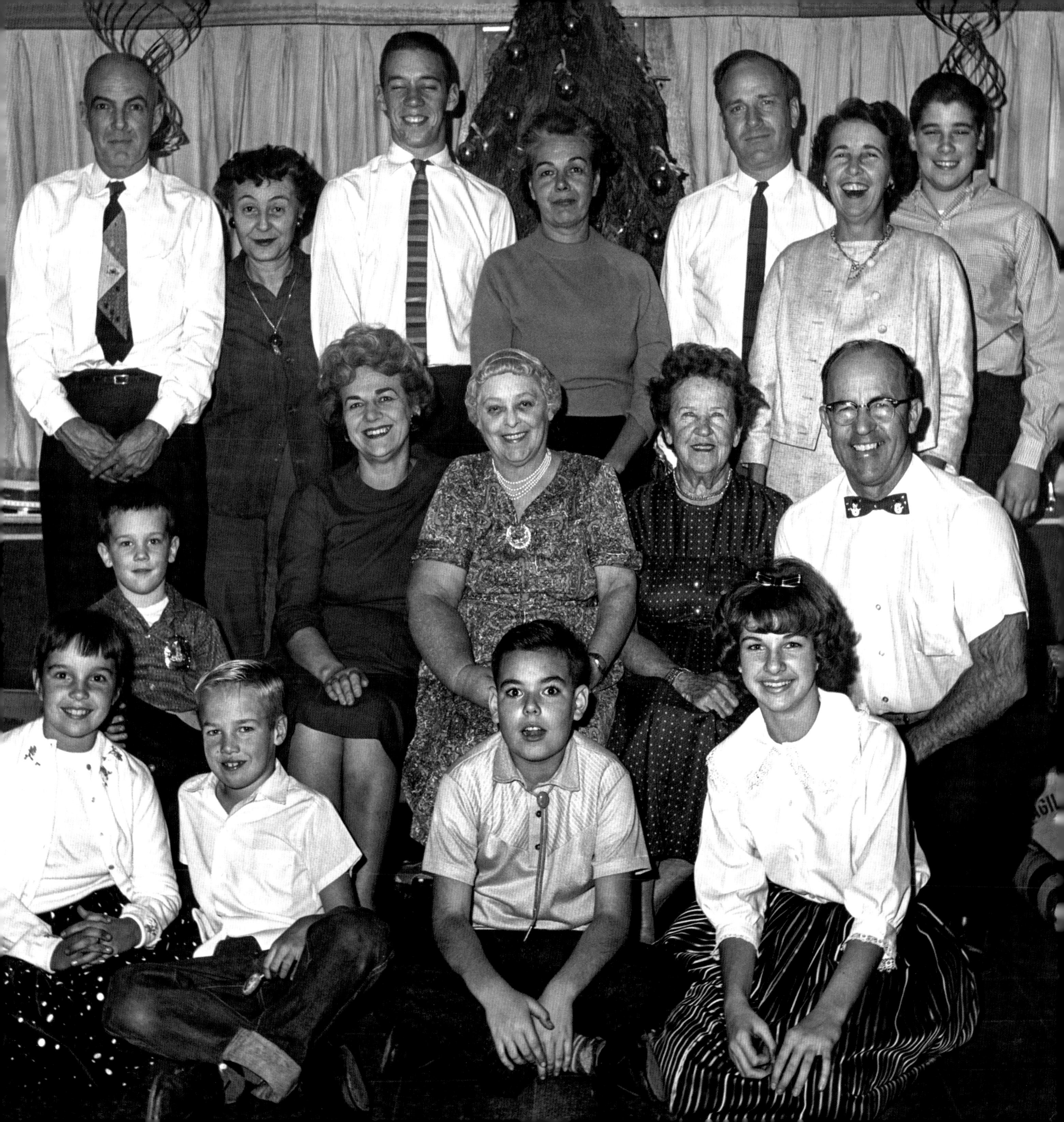

About the Artist

In his forty-five years as an artist, Gary Sweeney has established a body of artwork that is "as diverse in its media and presentation as it is singular in its wit and intelligence."[1]

Sweeney was born into the fertile artistic climate of 1950s Southern California, and both his father, aunt, and grandmother were artists. He graduated in 1975 with a degree in Fine Arts from UC Irvine, which was then a hotbed of Conceptualism and Post-Minimalism. To support his art making, which includes photography, painting, and sculpture—resulting in a body of work ranging from neon signs, billboards, and murals to rug making, book art, and video—Sweeney took a job as a baggage handler for Continental Airlines, from which he recently retired after thirty-five years; it provided steady income, insurance, and low-cost air travel.

After Sweeney transferred to Denver in 1982, he became an active member of the local alternative art scene. Shortly after, his art began focusing on personal experiences, especially the frequent family vacations of his youth. During that time, he took hundreds of snapshots of family and tourist destinations, which later found their way, appropriately captioned, onto large hand-tinted maps or greatly enlarged onto billboards. He also poured over family albums. From old photographs he created one series of work about his father's experiences as a police detective, and another about his parents' vacations "before the kids came along."

Gary Sweeney's humor is especially apparent in his public artwork scattered throughout the United States, most notably in Denver International Airport, San Antonio International Airport, The Green in Charlotte, North Carolina, and The Esplanade on Navigation in Houston, Texas.

Though he and his wife now live in San Antonio, Texas, Gary maintains a solid Southern California sensibility in both his art and manner. He remains, as one critic put it, "one of those rare artists who possesses both the necessary skill to create stylish work and the wit and intelligence to give substance to it."[2]

Jane Fudge
The View from Denver, exhibition catalogue, Kunsthistorisches Museum Wein, Vienna, Austria

1 Michael Paglia, "Pop Goes the Concept: The Art of Gary Sweeney," *Colorado Arts* (June 1994), 4.

2 Paglia, "Pop Goes the Concept," 4.

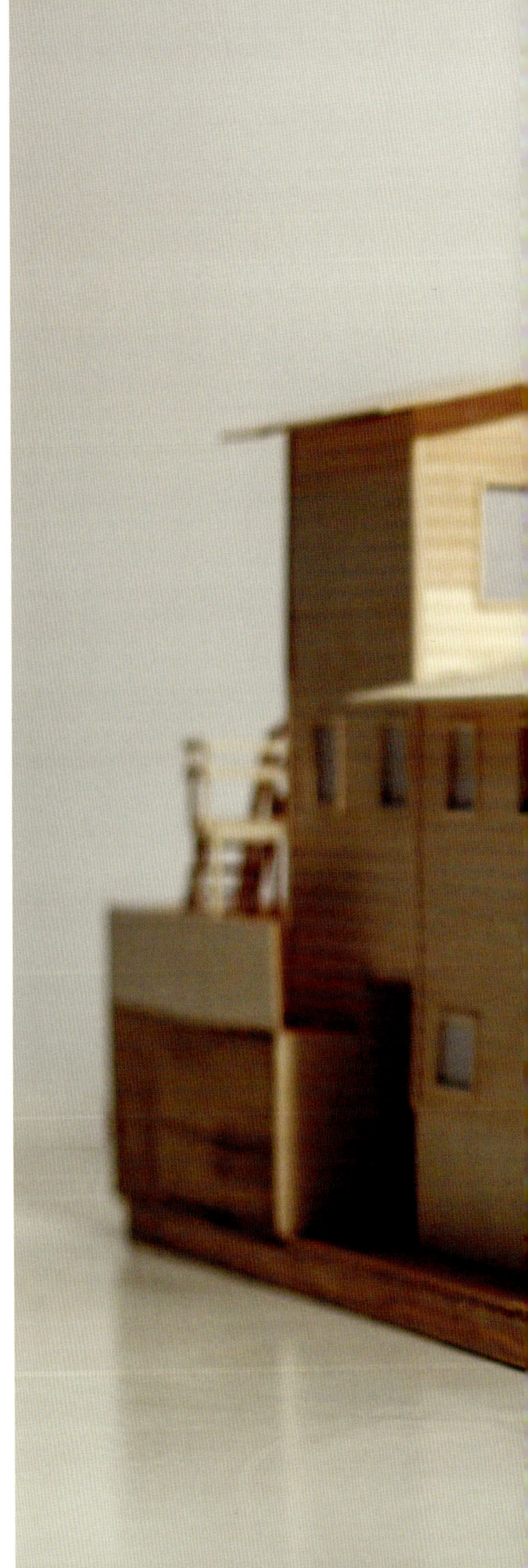

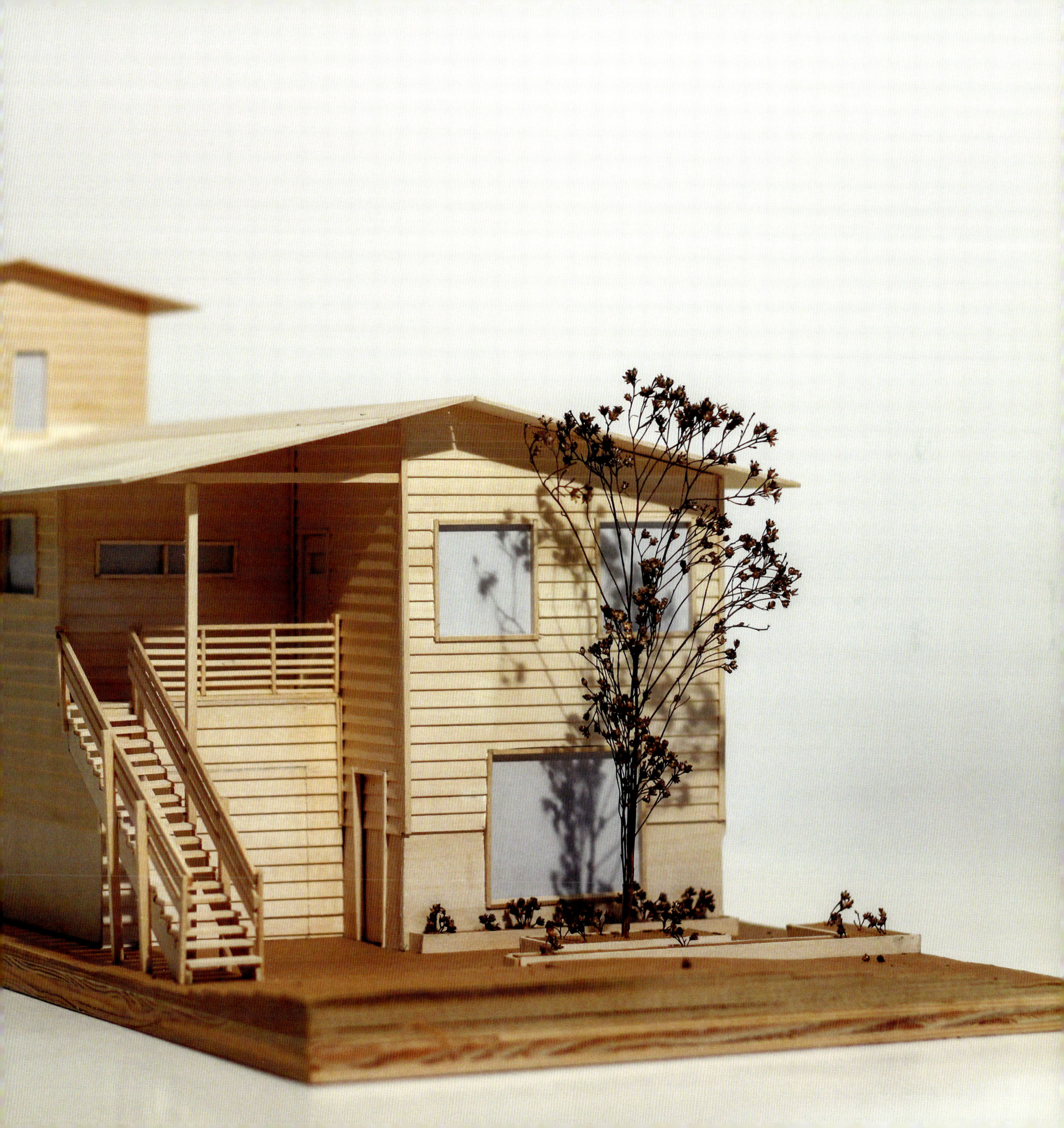

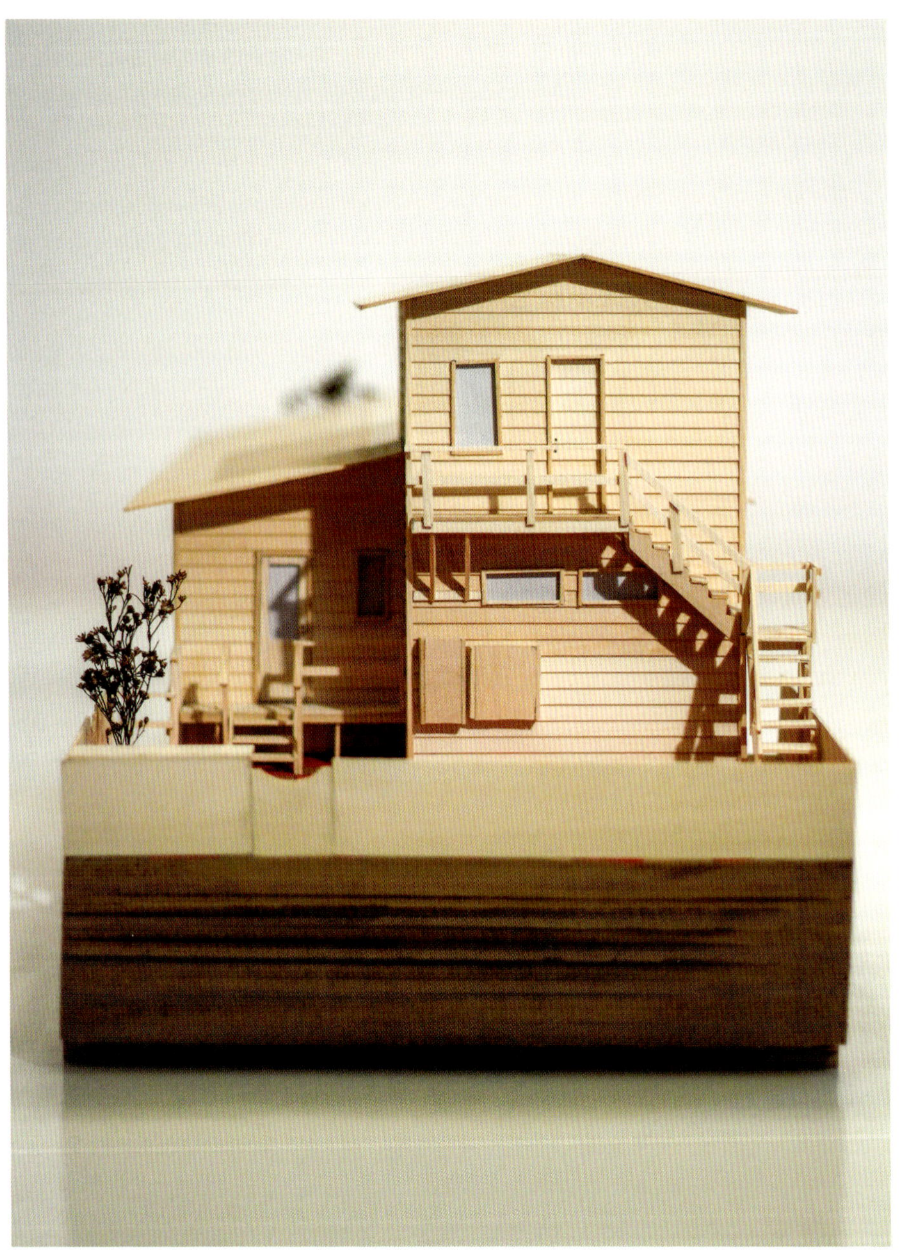

PREVIOUS & ABOVE » Scale model of the Sweeney home built by Trinidad Martinez after the house was demolished

Exhibition History

Selected Solo Exhibitions

2018 *A Manhattan Beach Memoir,* Blue Star Contemporary, San Antonio, TX

2014 *Rebus Puzzle,* Artpace Window Works, San Antonio, TX

2013 *Go West,* Parchman Stremmel Galleries, San Antonio, TX

Gary Sweeney: A Forty-Year Overview, Blue Star Contemporary, San Antonio, TX

2012 *Post-Obsessive,* Santa Reparata School of Art, Florence, Italy

2011 *Humor and Pathos,* Boulder Museum of Contemporary Art, Boulder, CO

If You Stand By Me, Three Walls, San Antonio, TX

2009 *Let This Be a Sign,* Unit B, San Antonio, TX

2008 *Loose Connections,* Big Medium, Austin, TX

Words of Wisdom, Art Guys Situation Room, Houston, TX

2007 *On This Site...,* Unit B, San Antonio, TX

2004 *Gary Sweeney,* Southwest School of Art, San Antonio, TX

2003 *The Story of Civilization,* Lawndale Art Center, Houston, TX

Word, University of Dallas Haggerty Gallery, Irving, TX

2002 *The Idiot,* Tokyo Project, Tokyo, Japan

Rough Draft, Robischon Gallery, Denver, CO

Signs of the Times, Blue Cube Gallery, Columbus, OH

2000 *A Project: The Story of Civilization,* Blue Star Contemporary, San Antonio, TX

1999 *Gary Sweeney,* Arizona Western College, Yuma, AZ

1998 *Across State Lines,* Parchman Stremmel Galleries, San Antonio, TX

Noir Series, Galveston Arts Center, Galveston, TX

1996 *Travels and Destinations,* Parchman Stremmel Galleries, San Antonio, TX

1993 *Learning About Culture,* Mackey Gallery, Denver, CO

1992 *Vacation '64,* Peyton Rule Gallery, Denver, CO

Selected Group Exhibitions

2018 *44 Texas Artists,* Louise Hopkins Underwood Center for the Arts, Lubbock, TX

2017 *Status? Prints from Puerto Rico to San Antonio, Texas,* Centro de Artes, San Antonio, TX

Storm Warning: Artists on Climate Change and the Environment, Vicki Myhren Gallery, University of Denver, Denver, CO

2014 *New Art/Arte Nuevo,* University of Texas at San Antonio, TX

2012 *Urban Decay,* Ravi Photo Gallery, Hyderabad, India

The West, New Delhi Art Center, New Delhi, India

2010 *The Brewery Invitational,* The Brewery Art Space, Los Angeles, CA

2009 *Art on the Green Outdoor Sculpture Invitational,* Kemp Center for the Arts, Wichita Falls, TX

The Great Texas Sculpture Roundup, Beeville Art Museum, Beeville, TX

2008 *Eco-Logic,* The Arts at Mark's Garage, Honolulu, HI

Eligible Traffic, Art Gallery Trinity University, San Antonio, TX

Texas Biennial 2008, Blue Star Contemporary, San Antonio, TX

2007 *Camp Marfa,* Old Fort Russell Building, Marfa, TX

Nexus, Texas, Contemporary Art Museum, Houston, TX

Texas Biennial 2007, Installation, East Cesar Chavez Blvd., Austin, TX

2006 *Decades of Influence,* Museum of Contemporary Art, Denver, CO

Horizons, Fowler Center, Arkansas State University, Jonesboro, AR

Crossing Borders: International Juried Exhibit, Laredo Center for the Arts, Laredo, TX

Word, Deborah Colton Gallery, Houston, TX

Juxtapositions, Alameda National Center for Latino Arts and Culture, San Antonio, TX

2003 *Neon Art in Texas,* Arts Alliance of Clear Lake, Clear Lake, TX

Spanglish, Artpace Hudson Showroom, San Antonio, TX

2002 *South Texas Outdoor Sculpture Exhibition,* International Sculpture, San Antonio, TX

2001 *The Wild West,* Arken Museum of Modern Art, Ishoj, Denmark

2001 Biennial Juried Exhibition, The McKinney Avenue Contemporary, Dallas, TX

1998 *Blue Star 8,* Blue Star Contemporary, San Antonio, TX

1997 *The View from Denver,* Kunsthistorisches Museum, Vienna, Austria

Una Casa Molt Particular, ACM, Mataro, Spain

1995 *The New American West,* Barcelona Project II, Barcelona, Spain

Scene Colorado/Sin Colorado, Denver Museum of Art, Denver, CO

1993 *Small Masterpieces*, Rule Modern and Contemporary, Denver, CO

Six Contemporary Artists from Colorado, FAD Barcelona, Barcelona, Spain

1992 *AAA+,* Gallery of Contemporary Art, University of Colorado, Colorado Springs, CO

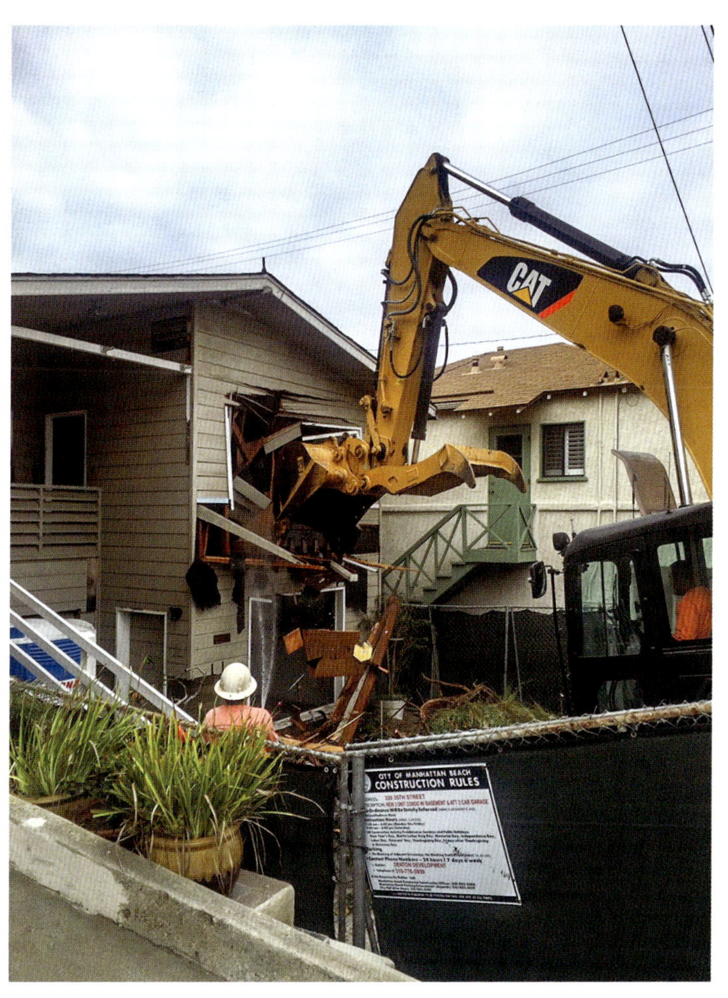
CAT
CITY OF MANHATTAN BEACH
CONSTRUCTION RULES

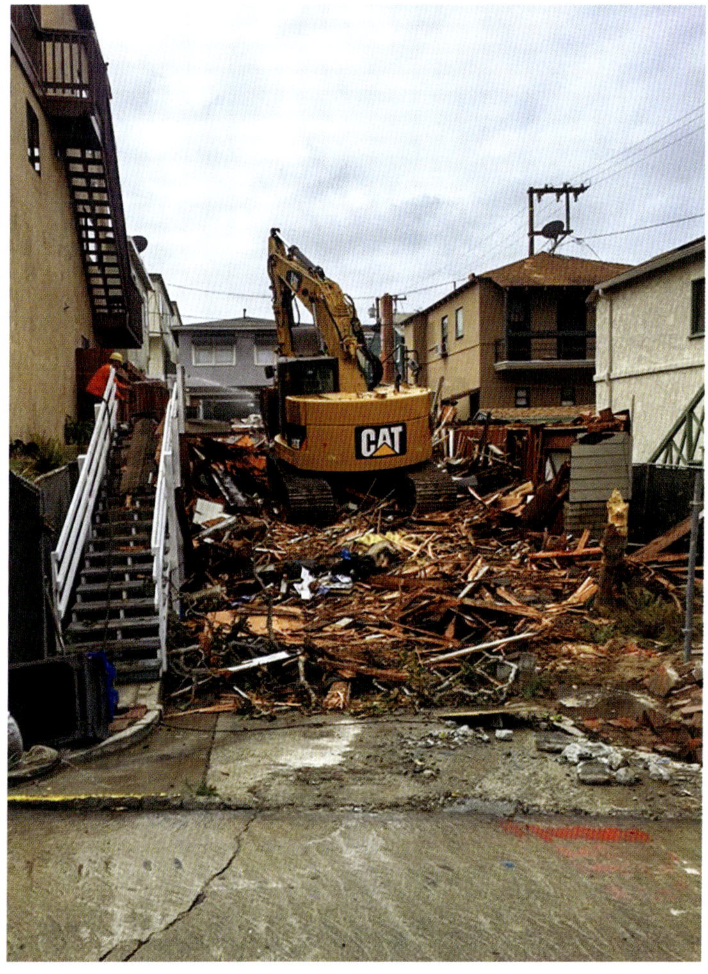
CAT

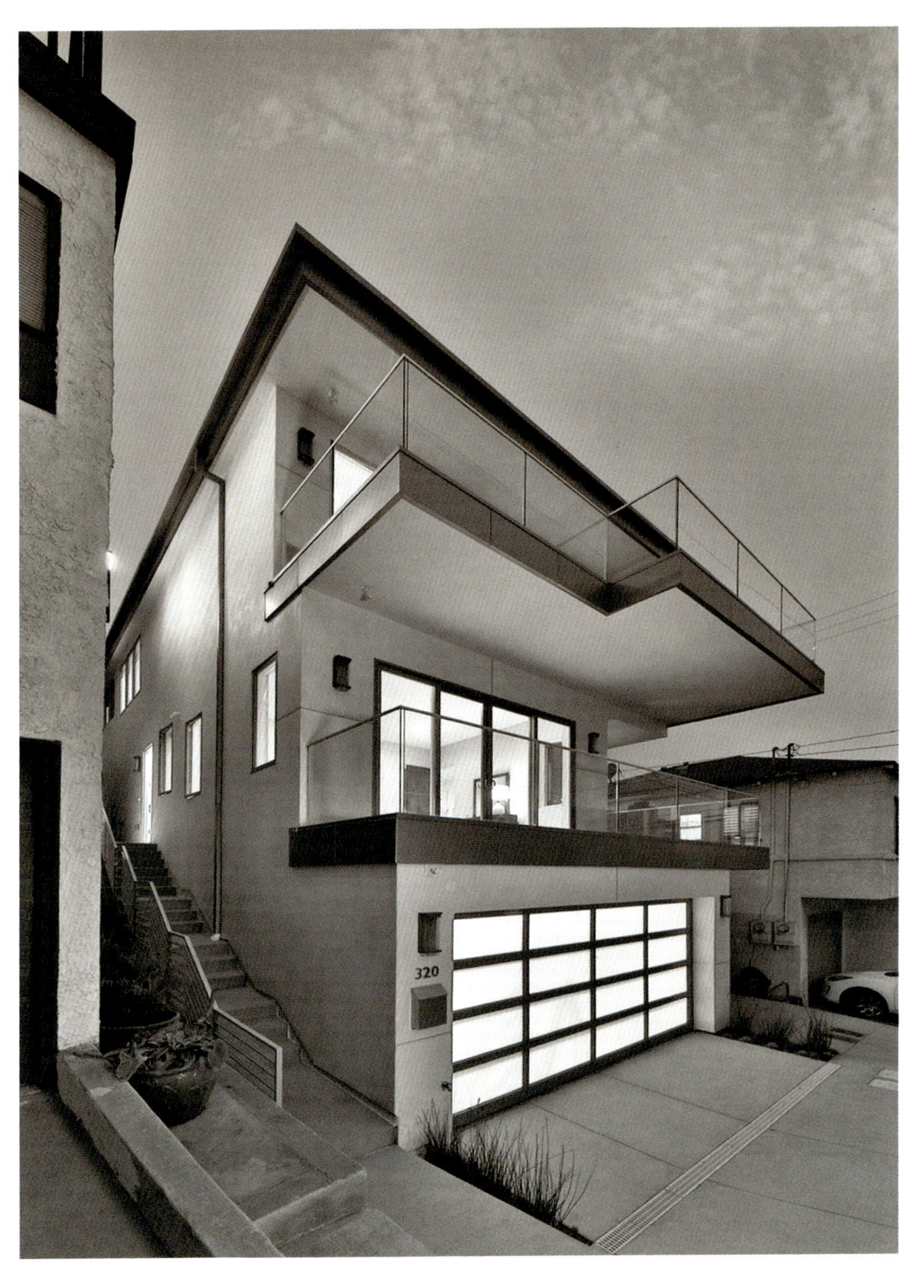

» New construction at 320 35th Street completed in 2017.

Acknowledgments

Thank you to Joe Kethan and Zach Slough for their hard work and dedication to making *A Manhattan Beach Memoir* possible. And thank you, Andréa, for your talent and patience in the design of this book. There must be some satisfaction in knowing that your ideas were always better than mine.